The Investor's Self-Teaching Seminars

UNDERSTANDING AND USING MARGIN

*The Investor's
Self-Teaching Seminars*

UNDERSTANDING AND USING MARGIN

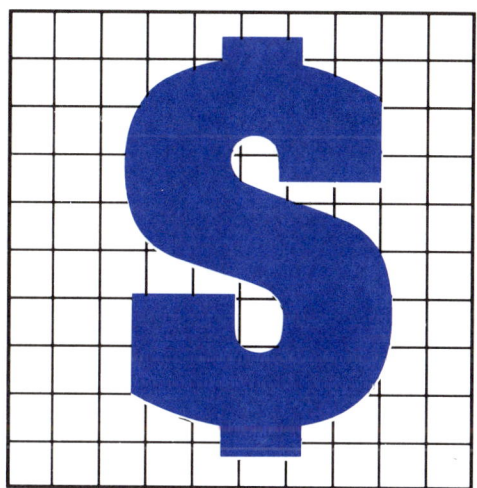

*One of a Series of Hands-On Workshops
Dedicated to the Serious Investor*

Michael T. Curley

PROBUS PUBLISHING COMPANY
Chicago, Illinois

© 1989 Michael T. Curley

ALL RIGHTS RESERVED. No part of this publication may be reproduced, stored in a retrieval system, or transmitted by any means, electronic, mechanical, photocopying, recording or otherwise, without the prior written permission of the publisher and the copyright holder.

This publication is designed to provide accurate and authoritative information in regard to the subject matter covered. It is sold with the understanding that the publisher is not engaged in rendering legal, accounting or other professional service.

Library of Congress Cataloging-in-Publication Data

Curley, Michael T.
    Understanding and using margin/Michael T. Curley.
       p. cm.—(The Investor's self-teaching seminars)
    ISBN 1-55738-084-8
    1. Margin accounts—United States. 2. Margin (Security trading)—United States. I. Title. II. Series
HG4963.C87 1989
332.64'5–dc20

Printed in the United States of America

1   2   3   4   5   6   7   8   9

CONTENTS

PREFACE	vii
CHAPTER ONE: CASH ACCOUNTS	**1**
Sale of Securities	5
Paying for Securities by the Sale of Other Securities	6
Delivery Against Payment	6
Chapter One Questions	8
CHAPTER TWO: INITIAL FEDERAL MARGIN REQUIREMENTS	**11**
Purchases	13
Sales	21
Chapter Two Questions	24
CHAPTER THREE: INITIAL AND MINIMUM MAINTENANCE REQUIREMENTS	**27**
Initial Requirements	30
House Requirements	31
NYSE Minimum Maintenance Requirements	31
Chapter Three Questions	38
CHAPTER FOUR: THE SPECIAL MEMORANDUM ACCOUNT	**41**
Customer's Account	48
Chapter Four Questions	59

CHAPTER FIVE: SHORT SALES — 61
- Covering of Short Sales — 71
- NYSE Minimum Maintenance Requirements — 72
- Sample Transactions — 74
- Short Sale Versus the Box or Short Against the Box — 76
- Chapter Five Questions — 82

CHAPTER SIX: BONDS — 85
- U.S. Government Securities — 89
- Zero-Coupon Government Obligations — 90
- Municipals — 92
- Nonconvertible Corporate Bonds — 95
- Chapter Six Questions — 98

CHAPTER SEVEN: MISCELLANEOUS CATEGORIES — 101
- When-Issued and When-Distributed Transactions — 103
- Marks to the Market — 106
- When-Distributed Securities — 107
- Segregation of Customer's Securities — 107
- Review of Customer's Accounts — 108
- Interest Charges — 110
- Margin on New Issues — 112
- Day Trades — 113
- Chapter Seven Questions — 117

APPENDIX A: THE FEDERAL RESERVE — 123
- Reserve Requirements — 126

APPENDIX B: ANSWERS TO CHAPTER QUESTIONS — 133
- Chapter One — 135
- Chapter Two — 136
- Chapter Three — 137
- Chapter Four — 138
- Chapter Five — 139
- Chapter Six — 140
- Chapter Seven — 140

APPENDIX C: GLOSSARY — 145

ABOUT THE AUTHOR — 159

Preface

PREFACE

Trading on margin has taken an unfair and unwarranted amount of abuse. Purchasing securities on margin is nothing more than purchasing securities on credit. Credit is not evil or bad and, if properly used, can be an extremely profitable means of investing.

If I told you that I had just purchased a house and paid for it in full, I am sure you would be surprised, because this is not the normal procedure for purchasing a house. Most people react to this statement by saying that (1) a house is a huge purchase requiring financing (true), and (2) there is no risk—real estate always increases in value (false).

I would be negligent not to tell you that any credit purchase of stocks, bonds, real estate, furniture, fixtures, etc., involves a degree of risk. However, a cash purchase in full of the same items involves the same degree of risk. The value of items purchased, whether financed or paid for in full, can decline giving you a loss. Real estate prices have dropped substantially in certain geographical areas such as Houston, Dallas, and Tulsa. These areas depend heavily on oil, and as the price of oil declined, these areas experienced a decline in jobs, increased unemployment and a decline in real estate value. The real estate decline affected houses being financed with a mortgage as well as those that were fully paid.

The first false notion one must discard is the idea that debt is bad. It is not. Borrowed funds used properly can result in considerable profits. The term *leveraged buyout* is very popular right now on Wall Street. It is nothing more than one company taking over another company with borrowed funds. Our economy and our standard of living as we know it today would not exist without credit.

The obvious fact in purchasing securities on credit, with the current requirements at 50 percent, is that one can purchase twice as much in a margin account as in a cash account. Consequently, if one purchases $10,000 worth of securities in a cash account and that security doubles in value, one has a profit of $10,000. The same $10,000 in a margin account enables one to purchase $20,000 in securities. Should these securities double in value, the profit is $20,000. That, in essence, is the principle behind margin trading.

Often, the complaint is voiced that an additional expense is involved in margin trading, because the broker charges interest on the money he is financing. And that is absolutely true. However, since one can purchase twice as many securities, twice as many dividends are available to offset a good portion of the interest charged.

A margin account can also be used to obtain financing for purposes other than buying and selling securities. Assume a customer has $40,000 in market value of listed securities and wants to buy a new car with a total sticker price of $17,000. Depositing these securities into a margin account, the broker is permitted to finance 50 percent, or $20,000. In this case, the customer has purchased his or her car and still maintained ownership of the securities. Interest charged by the broker is approximately the same as that charged by a bank for an auto loan. The advantage of the margin account is that the client does not have to make monthly payments to pay off the loan. The loan may be paid off at any time or can stay open indefinitely, provided the collateral is sufficient to meet the minimum maintenance requirement (this is discussed in detail in the text). In addition, the bank loan requires the automobile as collateral. The bank can thus dictate what kind of insurance must be purchased, whether alarms must be installed, etc. On the other

Preface

hand, with the margin account the loan is tied to the securities deposited and has nothing to do with the car.

While most margin accounts are longstanding accounts, many are opened and subsequently closed in a relatively short period of time. This is particularly true around April 15th of each year, when tax payments are due. Many times, securities are deposited and loans taken, the proceeds of which are used for the payment of taxes. Often these accounts are paid off and closed out relatively quickly.

At this point, a few comments should be made about margin trading risk. However, I first shall allay some of the misconceptions regarding two major crashes, October 29, 1929, and October 19, 1987.

One often hears that the 1929 crash was caused by margin trading. Although margin accounts were a factor, many other factors also came into play. To begin with, prior to the crash, no hard and fast margin requirements existed. The New York Stock Exchange had a *suggested* margin requirement of 20 percent. However, more often than not, customers were trading on 10 percent and in some cases 5 percent margin. This is clearly a case of too much credit. The sharp decline left many accounts in a deficit or close to no equity, forcing a liquidation. This has long since been rectified by the establishment of initial requirements (currently of 50 percent) and minimum maintenance requirements (currently 25 percent). As you can see, requirements are substantially higher now than in 1929.

The crash on October 19, 1987, was quite different. The stock market had changed substantially from 1929. Not only had the volume and the number of shares available increased, but new products had been introduced, such as equity options, broad-based index options, futures hedging strategies, program trading, and so-called *naked* writing of options, which can, at least in theory, result in unlimited loss.

Congress appointed a committee to look into the crash and come up with some suggestions to prevent a recurrence. As a result, margin requirements were increased on equity options, narrow- and broad-based index options, along with restrictions on program trading. No suggestion was made to increase either initial margin requirement of 50 percent or maintenance requirement of 25 percent.

As previously stated, there is risk in any investment. However, with knowledge of the product, diversification, and constant monitoring, risk can be greatly reduced. Certainly, there is nothing new in these concepts. However, an essential ingredient that is often overlooked is a thorough understanding of the vehicle (the margin account), which accommodates the purchasing and carrying of securities on margin. As of this writing, approximately 5,000,000 margin accounts exist, with debit balances in excess of $33 billion. The vast majority of these accounts are individual customers rather than institutional investors. I would venture to say that only a small percentage of customers who have margin accounts and the registered representatives servicing these accounts could get a passing grade on the exam at the back of this book.

ACKNOWLEDGEMENTS

The author acknowledges the valuable assistance of James R. Davis, Michelle D. Parsons, and Joseph A. Walker in the preparation of this volume.

Michael T. Curley

Chapter One

CASH ACCOUNTS

Most security transactions take place in a cash account. Regulation T of the Board of Governors of the Federal Reserve System (The Fed)[1], states that funds sufficient for the purchase of the securities should be in the account prior to the purchase. In the event funds are not on hand, there is an agreement between the broker and the customer that the customer will deposit the full cash payment "promptly."

Promptly is an important word. The Fed defines it to mean five (5) business days. Consequently, full cash payment should be received by the fifth business day—the settlement date. This would be an ideal or optimum situation, since the broker would be using the customer's money to pay for the purchase on the settlement date. The broker is required to pay the seller on the settlement date whether or not the customer paid for the purchase. If the customer has not paid by the settlement day, the broker would have to borrow from the bank, incurring an interest expense, which may not be passed on to the customer.

---

1 See Appendix A at the back of the book for a detailed discussion of the Federal Reserve System.

While the regulation states that payment should be received by the fifth business day, it goes one step further and states payment *must* be received no later than the seventh (7th) business day. As you can see, while payment received on the seventh business day satisfies Regulation T, the broker has incurred an expense of two days' interest charged by the bank. (The interest rate charged the broker by the bank is known as the broker's call rate.)

What happens in the event payment is not received by the seventh business day?

1. In the event an exceptional circumstance exists—e.g., customer called out of town unexpectedly or customer ill—the broker may (but is not required to) request an extension of time from one of the exchanges or the NASD.

    The extension of time is requested on a form giving the customer's name, the quantity, description of the security purchased, total dollar amount involved, the reason for the delay, number of days requested, and the customer's Social Security number.

    The request for an extension of time is submitted to the exchange or the NASD. If granted, the customer now has more time to pay. The maximum number of extensions which a customer can receive is five in any 12-month period.

2. Should payment not be received within the approved period, or if the extension was denied (or not requested), the broker would be required to: liquidate or sell out the customer's securities to raise the money to pay for this purchase.

At this point, what has happened in the customer's account? The proceeds of the sale have been used to pay for the purchase. This is a violation of Regulation T and the customer's account is *frozen* for the next 90 calendar days. The effect of this 90-day penalty is to require the customer to have sufficient funds on hand *prior* to any new purchase. No longer may the customer call the broker, purchase a security and then send in a check in payment.

Cash Accounts

Keep in mind that the Federal Reserve is concerned with the amount of credit outstanding. The cash account is specifically designed for customers wishing to buy and pay in full for their securities. By buying and selling without full cash payment the customer is in effect trading on 100 percent margin.

Regulation T also allows for an exception. Should a customer purchase a security one day and sell that very same security two days later, this customer's cash account would immediately become frozen for 90 calendar days. However, should the customer make full cash payment within seven business days, the restriction is automatically lifted. The Federal Reserve's reasoning is that, while the customer did buy and sell before making full cash payment, full cash payment (not just the difference between the purchase and the sale) was eventually made within the prescribed time. Should payment be received after the seventh business day, the broker must make written application to an exchange or NASD to have the freeze lifted.

SALE OF SECURITIES

The sale of a security in the customer's cash account has requirements similar to those for a purchase.

The securities to be sold should be held in the customer's account (long), or there is an agreement that the customer will deliver the security "promptly." Again, "promptly" is defined as five business days. This will enable the broker to deliver the security to the buying broker and obtain the payment.

Until January 15, 1973, the final settlement of the sale of a security was vague at best. Effective that date, the Securities Exchange Act of 1934 was amended to include Rule 15c 3-3-(M) and (N). This rule now requires that the sold securities be delivered no later than 10 business days after settlement. Should an exceptional circumstance arise, an extension of time may be requested from a national securities exchange or association such as the NASD. At the expiration of the extension, if the security is still not delivered, the broker is required to buy in the security. Unlike the purchase side, this would not freeze the account.

PAYING FOR SECURITIES BY THE SALE OF OTHER SECURITIES

If a security is to be paid for by the sale of another security, the sale should take place in time for sufficient funds to be on hand by the settlement date. Therefore, the purchase and the sale should be completed the same day.

The question now arises: what happens should a customer buy a security on day one and sell another security to pay for that purchase on day three? If such a transaction happened on a rare occasion, there would be no problem. However, the above transaction will cost the broker two days' interest, since the purchase transaction will settle two days before the funds become available. In addition, if such transactions occur with any degree of regularity, many firms, while not required to freeze the account for 90 days, impose such a restriction as a house policy. Infractions of this type should be monitored by the margin clerks and be brought to management's attention for corrective action. Keep in mind that these transactions are costly because of the interest being charged.

Normal settlement for equity and debt (exclusive of U.S. government obligations) instruments is five business days from the trade date. On occasion, if an individual requires immediate funds, such an arrangement may be accomplished by a *cash sale*. Such sales settle on the same day at 2:30 P.M. Any trade executed at 2:00 P.M. or after settles 30 minutes later.

DELIVERY AGAINST PAYMENT

Another type of transaction also takes place in the customer's cash account—the *C.O.D.* (Cash on Delivery) or *delivery versus payment*. This transaction is normally reserved for large institutional customers. However, any account could, at least in theory, transact business on this basis. The procedure works as follows.

When a customer purchases a security, the security is physically delivered to the customer, and the customer then pays for the purchase. Two conditions attach to such a transaction. First, the customer must advise the broker prior to the purchase that the method of payment is going to be delivery versus payment, and the broker must agree to the procedure. Second, in the event the broker is

Cash Accounts

unable to obtain the security to accomplish delivery, the broker has up to 35 calendar days to complete the delivery; i.e., if the broker is unable to obtain the security by the seventh business day, he is not obligated to liquidate the customer's account or obtain an extension of time. The broker has 35 calendar days from the trade date to accomplish delivery.

As a matter of information, transactions of this type normally settle on the fifth business day. This is so for two reasons. First, should delivery not be accomplished promptly, a good chance exists that the broker has part, but not all, of the securities for delivery. Consequently, the broker has paid for some of the securities out of his pocket, financed by a bank. Since a large portion of the broker's transactions are of this sort, special emphasis is placed on this area. Separate sections in the margin department only work on these types of transactions, insuring proper delivery instructions to the cashiers department. Second, there is an organization known as Depository Trust Company, which has immobilized many stock certificates, eliminating the physical movement of certificates from broker to bank or another broker.

Most institutional customers set up what are called *standing instructions* to deliver versus payment to a particular agent (usually a bank). The bank accepting the securities assigns an individual to handle and process the securities for this account. Anytime the institutional customer makes a purchase, a duplicate confirmation is sent to the receiving bank so it can anticipate that 1,000 shares of IBM will be delivered on settlement versus $110,000. Upon delivery, the bank will pay the broker.

Should the receiving agent be another broker, upon delivery of the security, the receiving broker must present the delivering broker with a *free funds* letter. This letter merely states that the funds for payment of this purchase do not represent the proceeds of sale of the security. Should the delivering broker not obtain this letter, the account must be frozen for 90 calendar days. As you can see, it would be extremely easy to buy at one broker and then sell at another and issue instructions to deliver versus payment. In order to prevent what is commonly referred to as *free riding*, a free funds letter must be obtained.

On occasion, delivery of securities is made and the delivery is rejected (DK'd). The receiving agent must attach a form called a DK (Don't Know) notice and advise the delivering party of the reason for rejection; e.g., delivery versus wrong amount of money, securities not in good delivery form, a mutilated coupon, or no knowledge of the trade. When this occurs, the 35-day period is immediately canceled and you must request an extension of time. The New York Stock Exchange will normally grant you two days to clear up this problem.

CHAPTER ONE QUESTIONS

1. Under Regulation T a purchase in a cash account must be paid for:
   a. by the settlement date.
   b. within seven business days.
   c. within seven calendar days.
   d. within five business days.

2. A cash account becomes frozen for 90 calendar days when a customer:
   a. pays for a purchase after the settlement date.
   b. sells a security and delivers it after the seventh business day.
   c. has been granted more than five extensions of time.
   d. buys a security and sells the same security and has not paid for it.

3. The Securities Act of 1934 requires a customer to deliver sold securities to the broker no later than:
   a. 10 calendar days after trade date.
   b. 10 business days after settlement date.
   c. 35 calendar days.
   d. 90 calendar days.

Cash Accounts

4. In order to qualify for a C.O.D. or D.V.P. transaction under Regulation T, the customer must issue instructions prior to the trade and:
   a. the securities cannot be obtained by the broker for delivery.
   b. request permission from the NYSE.
   c. request delivery after settlement date.
   d. there is no other requirement.

5. Extension of time may be requested from which organization:
   a. the Federal Reserve.
   b. the NYSE.
   c. the SEC.
   d. all of the above.

6. Extension of time should be requested:
   a. on the settlement date.
   b. on the seventh calendar day.
   c. on the seventh business day after the trade date.
   d. as soon as you know there will be a delay in payment.

7. A broker may remove a 90-day freeze if:
   a. the loss incurred is deposited by the seventh business day.
   b. under no circumstances.
   c. full cash payment is received by the seventh business day after purchase.
   d. the broker makes written application to the Federal Reserve Bank.

8. A *regular way* basis or settlement means the trade settles:
   a. 90 calendar days later.
   b. 35 calendar days later.
   c. on the seventh business day.
   d. on the fifth business day.

9. When a delivery of securities is DK'd, the rejecting broker must:
   a. do so the next business day.
   b. advise the delivering broker why the item is being DK'd.
   c. be rejected by the 35th calendar day.
   d. accept delivery if it is for less than $10,000.

10. A cash trade settles:
    a. on the fifth business day.
    b. the same day.
    c. on the seventh business day.
    d. at 2:30 P.M. on the next business day.

Chapter Two

INITIAL FEDERAL MARGIN REQUIREMENTS

PURCHASES

A margin transaction is essentially a credit transaction where the customer pays a portion of the purchase and the broker finances the balance. The amount that the broker is permitted to finance is controlled by the board of governors of the Federal Reserve under Regulation T. The amount that the broker is permitted to finance is currently 50 percent of the purchase price (the current market value). This amount is commonly referred to as the *Fed requirement*, *Reg. T requirement*, or the *initial requirement*.

Only *registered* securities may be purchased in the margin account. *Registered securities* means securities listed or traded on a national securities exchange—NYSE, AMEX, Philadelphia, Midwest, Pacific, or even the Honolulu Stock Exchange, or if the security appears on the OTC (over-the-counter) margin list published by the Federal Reserve. Also, an open-ended investment company that has been held a minimum of 30 days or unit investment trust that is registered under Section 8 of the Investment Company Act of 1940 may be carried in the margin account. In addition, effective November 13, 1984, Regulation T was amended to provide automatic margin status to any over-the-counter security that qualified for trading in the National Market System.

What happens when a customer purchases a security in a margin account? Anytime a customer purchases securities in a margin account the market value of the account is increased by the purchase and so is the debit balance. There are no exceptions. It is this increase in the customer's debit balance that causes what is commonly referred to as a *T call* or a *Fed call*. Remember the Federal Reserve requires a deposit of 50 percent of the purchase price of the security. The required margin deposit is due promptly. Prompt payment of the T or Fed call means the fifth business day and no later than the seventh business day. Requests for extensions are treated the same for both cash and margin transactions.

Suppose a customer purchases 100 shares of ABC for $10,000. (For illustration purposes, commissions, and interest charges have been eliminated.)

Market value	$10,000
Debit balance	10,000

Since this account started off with a zero balance, the market value is simply the price of the ABC shares. The debit balance represents the amount of money the customer owes the broker. At this point, the customer purchased $10,000 in securities and has not yet deposited any money.

The customer would then be issued a Fed call for $5,000 or 50 percent of the market value of the ABC shares. The actual format of the Fed call will vary from brokerage firm to brokerage firm. Some will have a very official-looking request giving the details of the transaction; others use a simple phone call from the broker.

In any event, assume in our case that the customer promptly deposits the required margin of $5,000. The account now looks like this:

Market value	$10,000
Debit balance	5,000
Equity	5,000

Initial Federal Margin Requirements

The money that the customer deposits reduces the debit balance by the amount of the deposit. Anytime money is deposited into a margin account, the debit balance is reduced by the amount of the deposit.

Equity represents the customer's ownership in the account. If the securities were sold and all debts were paid ($5,000 in our example), $5,000 would be left. This last $5,000 represents equity. Equity is computed by subtracting the debit balance from the current market value.

Market value	$10,000
Debit balance	−5,000
Equity	5,000

Why do people buy on margin? They are employing *financial leverage*. If you buy $5,000 in securities paying cash, and the security doubles in value, you have earned a $5,000 profit. That same $5,000 could be used by you to purchase $10,000 on margin. If that security doubles, you will have earned a $10,000 profit or twice as much. That, of course, is the bright side of margin buying. The dark side is that leverage on margin buying works both ways. With the margin account you can either double your gains or double your losses.

Getting back to our example, the customer's account is as follows:

Market value	$10,000
Debit balance	5,000
Equity	5,000

Let's assume that the value of the ABC shares increases to $12,000. The account would now look like this:

Market value	$12,000
Debit balance	5,000
Equity	7,000

Note: the market value changed to reflect the increase or the current market value. The debit balance remains unchanged. Keep in mind that the debit balance is the amount of money the customer owes the broker. There was no additional loan or extension of credit. Also note that the customer's equity changed in response to the increase in market value. Again, Equity = Market value − Debit balance.

Now we will compute our first margin computation. Remember, you are concerned with current market value versus current Regulation T requirement.

    Current market value $12,000
    Current Fed requirement   50%

Margin clerks have used the following tool for years to assist them in making the various margin computations:

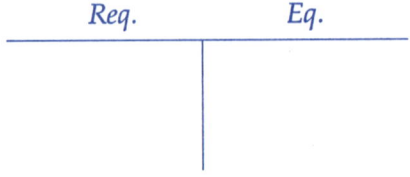

Draw a large "T" as shown, putting requirement (Req.) on one side and the equity (Eq.) on the other. Now you can take 50 percent of the current market value to get the Regulation T requirement.

$12,000 × 50% = $6,000 the current requirement

Market value − Debit balance = Equity
($12,000 − $5,000 = $7,000)

The equity is $7,000.

Req.	Eq.
$6,000	$7,000

Now subtract the requirement from the equity;

Req.	Eq.
$6,000	$7,000
	6,000
	$1,000 excess over Reg. T

Initial Federal Margin Requirements

The $1,000 is known as *excess over Regulation T*. Excess means extra, something not required. Question: If it is extra or not required, may I have it?—and the answer is yes.

Now, if the customer requests and receives a check for the $1,000, the account will appear as follows:

Market value	$12,000
Debit balance	6,000
Equity	6,000

Note: Sending the customer $1,000 increases the debit balance. This is because the broker loaned the customer an additional $1,000 based on the current value of the collateral, which is now worth $12,000. This additional $1,000 loan is permissible under Regulation T.

When referring to margin and margin accounts, we often think of a two-sided account. On one side, the customer side, there is a requirement to have 50 percent of the market value on deposit. On the other side, the broker side, the potential exists to lend the customer up to 50 percent of the market value. Therefore, in the above example the broker was able to and did lend the customer an additional $1,000.

As stated earlier, anytime money is *deposited* into the customer's account, regardless of the reason, the debit balance is *decreased*. It would stand to reason, then, that anytime funds are *withdrawn*, the debit balance would be *increased* by that amount. In the above example the customer withdrew $1,000; consequently, the debit balance was increased by the amount of the withdrawal.

While a withdrawal of $1,000 is permissible, the $1,000 excess can be converted into *buying power*. Buying power means the amount of securities you can purchase without depositing any additional funds. With a 50 percent Regulation T requirement, all you do to find the buying power is double the excess (multiply by 2):

Req.	*Eq.*	
$6,000	$7,000	
	6,000	
	$1,000	excess over Reg. T
	×2	
	2,000	buying power

If the customer purchases $2,000 of listed securities in his/her account, the account will appear as follows:

Market value	$14,000
Debit balance	7,000
Equity	7,000

Note: The market value increased by the value of the securities purchased—$2,000. Also, the debit balance was increased by the full purchase price. Why? Because the customer just purchased securities valued at $2,000 and has not paid for them. Keep in mind that there is another side to the transaction—someone sold the customer $2,000 worth or securities. If the customer did not pay for them, the broker would have to finance the entire purchase. Therefore, this additional loan is reflected as an increase in the customer's debit balance in this situation. The customer used the excess equity and did not have to make a deposit in the account. As a result of this transaction, the account is now at exactly 50 percent:

Market value	$14,000
Debit balance	7,000
Equity	7,000

Any additional purchases at this point would require the necessary 50 percent deposit. Should this customer purchase another $5,000 in listed securities, the account would appear as follows:

Market value	$19,000
Debit value	12,000
Equity	7,000

A Reg. T call for 50 percent of $5,000 ($2,500) would be issued and should be answered promptly (five business days). If the customer deposits the funds within the prescribed time, the margin account would now appear as follows:

Market value	$19,000
Debit balance	9,500
Equity	9,500

Initial Federal Margin Requirements

Again, funds were received into the account, therefore, the equity was increased and the debit balance was reduced by the deposited amount.

The Federal Reserve's requirement of 50 percent is also known as an "initial" requirement and would not come into effect again until there was an additional purchase. This purchase would, of course, trigger a new initial requirement of 50 percent of the purchase price.

Up to this point, we have discussed only the effects on a margin account when the price of the securities increase in market value. Excess is created and buying power established. What happens when there is a decline in market value?

Our account now looks like this:

Market value	$19,000
Debit balance	9,500
Equity	9,500

If the market value were to decline to $17,000, the account would change accordingly:

Market value	$17,000
Debit balance	9,500
Equity	7,500

Note: The market value changed to reflect the decrease in the price of the securities. The debit balance remains unchanged—the client still owes the broker $9,500. The equity decreased in response to the decrease in market value. Remember, Equity = Market value − Debit Balance.

This margin account is now known as a restricted margin account. This is not to be confused with a cash account on a 90-day restriction or freeze. A restricted margin account means that the customer's equity is below the current Federal Reserve margin requirement of 50 percent. The restriction actually applies to the broker, who may not lend the customer any additional funds. In our account, the Regulation T requirement is 50% × $17,000 = $8,500, yet the current equity is only $7,500.

Req.	Eq.
$8,500	$7,500

In this case, the requirement exceeds the equity in the customer's account.

Does this mean that the customer is prohibited from purchasing additional securities? Absolutely not. Most active margin accounts are in fact *restricted* margin accounts. The margin trader will buy additional securities with any excess over Regulation T. Therefore, should the market have a sell off, the market value would go down, reducing his equity and thereby restricting the account. A restricted margin account carries no bad connotation. The broker merely cannot lend the customer additional funds as the account stands. Any new purchases will require a 50 percent deposit, and the broker may extend credit for these new purchases. In the event this customer purchases additional securities of $6,000, his account would appear as follows:

Market value	$23,000 (increased by $6,000)
Debit balance	15,500 (increased by $6,000)
Equity	7,500 (unchanged)

The customer would get a Reg. T call for 50 percent of the purchase price ($3,000). When the customer deposits the required $3,000 promptly, the account would change to:

Market value	$23,000 (unchanged)
Debit balance	12,500 (decreased by $3,000)
Equity	10,500 (increased by $3,000)

Note: After the deposit of the required margin, this account is still classified as a restricted margin account. It is not necessary to bring the entire account back up to 50 percent margin. The customer was required only to deposit 50 percent of the last purchase.

Initial Federal Margin Requirements

SALES

Thus far our examples and discussion have been about purchases. Sales of securities in a margin account are the exact opposite of purchases.

Let's go back to our margin account:

Market value	$23,000
Debit balance	12,500
Equity	10,500

If this customer sold $5,000 of securities, the account would look like this:

Market value	$18,000
Debit balance	7,500
Equity	10,500

The market value would be reduced by the proceeds of sale—$5,000. The debit balance would also be reduced by $5,000. The debit balance is reduced by the full amount, because the broker actually received the proceeds of sale, since the broker is holding the securities as collateral. While the customer is the owner of the securities, they are usually held in the name of the broker or his nominee (street name).

When a sale of securities occurs, 50 percent of the proceeds of the sale may be released to the customer (the reverse of a purchase requiring a deposit).

Here is the customer's account after the sale but prior to the release of any of the proceeds:

Market value	$18,000
Debit balance	7,500
Equity	10,500

If the customer was sent a check for $2,500, 50% of $5,000, the account would change to:

Market value	$18,000
Debit balance	10,000
Equity	8,000

As previously stated, anytime money comes into the margin account, the debit balance is reduced. Anytime money leaves the account, the debit balance is increased. A further look at this account also reveals that after the permissible withdrawal, the margin account is still classified as a restricted margin account.

Fifty percent or market value is $9,000. The customer's equity is only $8,000.

Req.	*Eq.*
$9,000	$8,000

Up to this point, the customer has met the Fed or Reg. T calls by depositing money. Which is quite common. However, there are other methods of meeting a margin call.

In addition to having a 50 percent requirement on purchases, listed and over-the-counter marginable securities also have *loan value*. If a customer deposited fully paid for marginable securities, the broker would be permitted to lend the customer 50 percent of their current market value. Therefore, a Reg. T call could be satisfied with a deposit of securities valued at two times the call.

Suppose our customer now makes an additional purchase of $7,000. The account would look like this:

Market value	$25,000
Debit balance	17,000
Equity	8,000

and there would be an outstanding Reg. T call of $3,500. The customer could deposit marginable securities worth $7,000 to satisfy the Reg. T call (50% × $7,000 = $3,500).

After the deposit of the securities, the account would now look like this:

Initial Federal Margin Requirements

Market value	$32,000
Debit balance	17,000
Equity	15,000

Note: The market value and the equity increased by the value of securities deposited, but no change was made to the customer's debit balance. Deposits of securities will only affect the market value and equity in an account. The debit balance is the amount owed to the broker and will be reduced only by depositing monies.

Another way of meeting a margin call is through the sale of other securities. As was the case in the cash account, in a margin account sales of securities to pay for purchases should be placed on the same day, so that the settlement dates coincide. If a customer purchases $7,000 and sells $7,000 of securities on the same day, no change occurs in the customer account. However, it is unusual to come out exactly even. Often, there is a slight difference. If there were a purchase of $7,500 and a sale of $7,300, the purchase would exceed the sale by $200, requiring a T call of $100—50 percent of the difference. In this regard, Regulation T has the provision that calls not in excess of $500 may be waived at the option of the broker. In the event the sale takes place after the trade date of the purchase, the account is said to be meeting the margin call by liquidation. An occasional liquidation is at best tolerated. The NYSE has stated through interpretation of its margin rules that "a practice of meeting margin calls by liquidation is prohibited." What constitutes "a practice"? This is subject to interpretation based on the number of transactions the customer makes.

The last way to meet a Reg. T call, and perhaps the least likely to occur is by market appreciation. Here is an example:

Market value	$100,000
Debit balance	52,000
Equity	48,000
Buy 100 ABC @ 20	$2,000
Reg. T call	$1,000

Margin account after purchase:

Market value	$102,000
Debit balance	54,000
Equity	48,000

Should the market value of the margin account increase between the trade date and settlement date (five business days) to $108,000 or more, the $1,000 Reg. T margin call will be considered answered. With the market value at $108,000 and the debit at $54,000, equity would be at exactly 50 percent, requiring no additional funds.

Market value	$108,000	Req.	Eq.
Debit balance	54,000	$54,000	$54,000
Equity	54,000		

To summarize, there are four ways to meet a Federal margin call:

1. Deposit the required funds.
2. Sell a security of equal or greater value than the security purchased.
3. Deposit securities having loan value equal to or greater than the margin call.
4. By market appreciation.

CHAPTER TWO QUESTIONS

1. Excess Over Regulation T is:
    a. the amount that is required as a result of purchases in a customer's margin account.
    b. the amount a broker may finance as a result of a purchase of listed securities.
    c. the amount of money in excess of Regulation T that may be withdrawn from the account or used to purchase additional securities.
    d. all of the above.

2. The amount of money that the broker finances is called:
   a. current market value.
   b. excess over Regulation T.
   c. equity.
   d. debit balance.

3. Loan Value is:
   a. the market value of all securities in an account.
   b. the amount of the customer's debt.
   c. the amount of money that may be loaned to the customer based on the value of listed securities.
   d. a good faith deposit.

4. A Regulation T call must be met within:
   a. seven business days after the trade date.
   b. five business days after the trade date.
   c. the next business day.
   d. 35 calendar days.

5. A Regulation T call may be answered by:
   a. a deposit of money.
   b. a deposit of securities with sufficient loan value.
   c. liquidation.
   d. all of the above.

6. The initial Regulation T requirement is 50 percent, and the account has a long market value of $40,000 and a debit balance of $12,500. The Regulation T excess is:
   a. $750.
   b. $7,500.
   c. $10,000.
   d. $15,000.

7. (Same account as in Question 6.) The buying power in this account is:
   a. $1,500.
   b. none.
   c. $15,000.
   d. $20,000.

8. Customer's account is as follows, and Regulation T is at 50 percent.

Market value	25,000
Debit balance	15,000
Equity	10,000

   This account is:
   a. a cash account.
   b. a restricted margin account.
   c. in deficit.
   d. a restricted cash account.

9. (Same account as in Question 8.) The customer purchases $8,500 of listed securities. After the purchase the debit balance will:
   a. remain the same.
   b. be $23,500.
   c. be $19,250.
   d. be $10,750.

10. (Same account as in Question 9.) This account will be on call for:
    a. $10,000.
    b. $16,750.
    c. $8,500.
    d. $4,250.

Chapter Three

INITIAL AND MINIMUM MAINTENANCE REQUIREMENTS

Thus far, we have discussed the initial requirements of the Federal Reserve Board. What happens after the margin account has been opened and the required margin deposited? As far as the Federal Reserve is concerned, its job was finished when the initial requirement was set and satisfied. If the market value of the securities went to zero, it would be of no concern to the Federal Reserve. On the other hand, not only would the customer be in a precarious position, but also the broker, since he is financing the transaction.

To prevent the broker from having an account become an unsecured debit, the NYSE[1] as well as the regional exchanges and the NASD have established initial and minimum *maintenance* requirements

---

[1] The margin rules of the New York and regional stock exchanges and the NASD are identical. Further discussion of maintenance requirements will refer only to the NYSE rules.

INITIAL REQUIREMENTS

The initial equity requirement to open or trade in a margin account is $2,000. Therefore, a customer wishing to open an account using the maximum financing (50 percent) and the minimum initial deposit would have to purchase $4,000 market value of securities. The account would then look like this:

Market value	$4,000
Debit balance	2,000
Equity	2,000

Purchase of a lesser amount—say $3,000—would still require an initial deposit of $2,000, even though this exceeds the Regulation T requirement of 50 percent.

A purchase of $1,800 in a new margin account would require only $1,800. A broker would never ask a customer to deposit more than the full cost of the security.

The initial requirements of the NYSE are exactly that—initial requirements. The $2,000 does not have to be maintained. In our first example, the customer's account looked like this:

Market value	$4,000
Debit balance	2,000
Equity	2,000

If the market value declined to $3,000, the customer's account would appear thus:

Market value	$3,000
Debit balance	2,000
Equity	1,000

This account is in compliance with the NYSE rules and in satisfactory condition. While the equity is now below $2,000, this was occasioned by market activity and not by a withdrawal of funds. However, if this customer now wished to purchase $1,000 of listed securities, this transaction would be subject to the NYSE $2,000 requirement. He would, therefore, be required to deposit the full $1,000, as opposed to the $500 Regulation T requirement.

Initial and Minimum Maintenance Requirements

The customer's account after the purchase and $1,000 deposit would now appear as:

Market value	$4,000
Debit balance	2,000
Equity	2,000

HOUSE REQUIREMENTS

The rules of the NYSE and the Federal Reserve are minimum requirements and brokers may (and most do) have *house requirements* in excess of the NYSE and Federal Reserve minimums. This is fine, as long as the house requirements are not lower than these minimum requirements. One firm has a house requirement of $250,000 to open a margin account. Obviously, this broker is interested in a select group of customers.

The balance of this chapter will explain in detail the NYSE minimum maintenance requirement on long positions (securities owned). Keep in mind that many firms have house requirements in excess of these minimums and in fact, they vary from broker to broker.

NYSE MINIMUM MAINTENANCE REQUIREMENTS

The NYSE, in addition to the initial requirement, has a minimum maintenance requirement that the customer's equity in the account must be equal to at least 25 percent of the market value of the securities.

As an example, assume a customer purchases $10,000 of listed securities and deposits the required 50 percent ($5,000) into the account.

Market value	$10,000
Debit balance	5,000
Equity	5,000

If the market value declines to $8,000, how does the customer's account stand in regard to the NYSE minimum maintenance requirement? The procedure for determining this is similar to that of recomputing the account for buying power. The only difference is the requirement for 25 percent as opposed to 50 percent.

Market value	$8,000
Debit balance	5,000
Equity	3,000

At this point, calculate 25 percent of the current market value:

$$25\% \times \$8,000 = \$2,000$$

Req.	Eq.	
$2,000	$3,000	
	2,000	
	$1,000	excess over NYSE maintenance requirement

As you can see, the requirement is $2,000 versus an equity of $3,000, leaving an excess of $1,000. This excess cannot be withdrawn or converted into buying power, since it is only excess over the NYSE minimum maintenance requirement. This means that this account could withstand even further market deciine without incurring a maintenance call.

Suppose the market value declines further to $6,000. How would the account stand?

Market value	$6,000
Debit balance	5,000
Equity	1,000

Maintenance Requirement = 25% × $6,000 = $1,500

Req.	Eq.
$1,500	$1,000

We now have a situation where the requirement exceeds the customer's equity. If you subtract the equity from the requirement,

Initial and Minimum Maintenance Requirements 33

this will tell you how much the customer must deposit to bring the account back into compliance with the NYSE maintenance requirement.

	Req.	*Eq.*
	$1,500	$1,000
	1,000	
NYSE maintenance call	500	

This customer would be contacted to deposit at least $500.

Just like a Federal call, a NYSE maintenance call may be answered in any of four ways:

1. Depositing the required funds.
2. By liquidation (selling securities).
3. Depositing additional securities.
4. Market appreciation.

Should the customer answer the maintenance call by depositing money, the effect on the account would be:

Market value	$6,000
Debit balance	4,500
Equity	1,500

The deposit of the money will reduce the debit balance and increase the equity by $500. Remember, anytime money is deposited into the margin account the debit balance is reduced and the equity is increased by the amount of the deposit, regardless of the reason.

Req.	*Eq.*
$1,500	$1,500

The account is now in compliance with NYSE rules. As this account is right on the line, most brokers would ask for more funds.

In the event the customer does not want to deposit the additional funds but wishes to sell out securities, simply multiply the amount of the maintenance call by 4:

Market value	$6,000
Debit balance	5,000
Equity	1,000

	Req.	Eq.
	$1,500	$1,000
	1,000	
NYSE maintenance call	500	

The NYSE call is $500. $500 × 4 = $2,000. This customer must sell $2,000 in securities to bring the account back into compliance with NYSE rules.

After the sale, the account would appear thus:

Market value	$4,000
Debit balance	3,000
Equity	1,000

The sale of $2,000 reduces the market value and the debit balance by $2,000. Recompute the account and see how the account stands from the NYSE maintenance requirements. Twenty-five percent of the new current market value: 25% × $4,000 = $1,000.

Req.	Eq.
$1,000	$1,000

The account is back in compliance with the NYSE maintenance requirements.

Initial and Minimum Maintenance Requirements

Another way of meeting the NYSE call is by depositing additional collateral using the same account:

Market value	$6,000
Debit balance	5,000
Equity	1,000

Once again, the account is on NYSE call for $500.

Let's say the customer wanted to meet the call by bringing in additional collateral. What is the minimum market value of securities that must be deposited? To determine the amount, simply multiply NYSE call amount by 4/3. On the account above:

$$4/3 \times \$500 = \frac{2000}{3} = \$666$$

The customer would have to deposit securities with a market value of $666.

Why couldn't the customer bring in just $500 worth of securities? Once the additional collateral is received into the account, those securities become subject to the NYSE 25 percent maintenance requirement. Consequently, the additional collateral is needed to bring the entire account up to 25 percent. After the deposit of the additional collateral, the account would now appear as follows:

Market value	$6,666
Debit balance	5,000
Equity	1,666

The deposit of the additional collateral will increase the market value and the customer's equity. However, this additional collateral in no way affects the customer's debit balance. If you recompute the account now, you will see that the account meets the NYSE minimum maintenance requirements:

$$25\% \times \$6,666 = \$1,666$$

The last way of meeting a NYSE maintenance call would be through market appreciation. This would happen if the market value increased in a relatively short period of time to the point where the account would meet the NYSE minimum requirements. We can determine the price the securities would have to rise to by simply multiplying 4/3 the debit balance.

$$4/3 \times \$5,000 = \$6,666$$

Therefore, should the market value of the securities in the account increase to $6,666, the account would meet the NYSE minimum maintenance requirements. Allowing for the meeting of the call by market appreciation is at the discretion of the broker. Many brokers will not allow it. The reasoning is that market fluctuations will cause the customer to be on call one day, off the next. It becomes difficult to keep track of the fluctuations, and the chance for error and violation of the rules multiplies.

Thus far when looking at the NYSE minimum maintenance requirements, we have looked only at the customer's margin account. Suppose the customer also has a cash account and has securities in it. The securities held in the customer's cash account may also be used to supply the necessary margin. The safest way to make this happen is to transfer the securities from the cash account to the margin account. However, the customer may not want to do this. In fact, the securities may not be eligible for the margin account. Many over-the-counter securities are not permitted in the customer's margin account nor do they have loan value.

However, these securities have value from the standpoint that they can be sold. Using our account, assume the customer also has a cash account with $6,000 market value of non-marginable over-the-counter securities.

Cash Account		Margin Account	
Market value	$6,000	Market value	$6,000
		Debit balance	5,000
		Equity	1,000

Initial and Minimum Maintenance Requirements

Recompute for NYSE minimum maintenance requirements:

Req.	Eq.
$1,500	$1,000
1,000	6,000
500	$7,000

In this example, we used 25 percent of the current market value in the margin account ($6,000 × 25% = $1,500) and its equity of $1,000. Now look at the cash account. To use the customer's cash account to support his margin account, the equity in the cash account must be compared to the same margin requirements as those in the margin account. This is why there is an additional $1,500 under the requirement side (25% × $6,000 = $1,500). Note that the full market value of $6,000 is used on the equity side. Since there is never a debit balance in the cash account, the equity is the same amount as the market value. Therefore, the customer has a total requirement of $3,000 versus a total equity of $7,000. There is now an excess in the combined accounts, so there would be no NYSE minimum maintenance call. Keep in mind that while we are looking to the cash account to support the margin account, the securities must remain in the cash account.

A variation of the above is known as a *guaranteed account*. This is a situation where one account supports another, but the accounts belong to different individuals. For instance, a husband might guarantee his wife's account or vice versa; or a father might guarantee his child's account. If such a situation exists, the guarantee must be in writing and should state the dollar amount or limit of the guarantee.

J. Jones Margin Account		W. Smith Margin Account	
Market value	$40,000		$6,000
Debit balance	17,000		5,000
Equity	23,000		1,000

Req.	Eq.	
$ 1,500	$ 1,000	Smith account
10,000	23,000	Jones account
$11,500	$24,000	Combined

The above accounts were simply combined to see how they stand on a combined basis. Mr. Smith's account is under-margined, but when combined with Mr. Jones' account, both would satisfy the NYSE requirements.

A word of caution: guarantees should be checked on a regular basis to ensure they are still in effect. Should Mr. Jones cancel his guarantee, Mr. Smith would have a call for $500.

How much time does a customer have to meet a maintenance call? Rule 431 of the NYSE sets the maximum time limit as 15 business days from the date the account went below the NYSE limits. Fifteen business days is a very long time, and most firms would not go along with that amount of time. However, maintenance calls are different than T calls in this regard. A customer who purchases securities knows he must pay for them within a specified period of time. The customer makes his commitment at the time he purchases securities.

A maintenance call is occasioned by market activity. This may be a longstanding customer who has just had the market go against him. Under these circumstances, a firm may want to extend the time for the client to the time limit permissible.

CHAPTER THREE QUESTIONS

1. A maintenance call is:
    a. a request for funds as a result of a purchase.
    b. that amount required when the margin account is initially opened.
    c. also called a Regulation T call.
    d. a request for funds when market changes decrease an account's equity below the broker's maintenance requirements.

Initial and Minimum Maintenance Requirements 39

2. The New York Stock Exchange's minimum maintenance requirement for long positions is:
   a. 25 percent of the market value.
   b. 50 percent of the market value.
   c. 25 percent of the equity in a customer's account.
   d. 50 percent of the debit balance.

3. Excess over NYSE minimum maintenance is:
   a. the amount by which the loan value exceeds the maintenance requirements.
   b. the amount by which the loan value exceeds the debit balance.
   c. the amount the account's equity exceeds the maintenance requirement.
   d. the amount over the Regulation T requirement.

4. Excess over NYSE minimum maintenance may:
   a. be withdrawn.
   b. be used to purchase additional securities.
   c. not be withdrawn.
   d. none of the above.

5. A customer opens a margin account with an initial transaction of a purchase of 100 ABC @ 24. Regulation T requirements are 50 percent. The customer must deposit:
   a. $1,200.
   b. $2,400.
   c. $1,000.
   d. $2,000.

6. Customer's margin account is as follows:

Market value	$18,000
Debit balance	13,900
Equity	4,100

   This account is under NYSE minimum maintenance requirements by:
   a. $4,900.
   b. $400.

c. $2,000.
d. $500.

7. (Same account as in Question 6.) The customer wishes to meet the call by liquidation, the customer must sell:
   a. $1,600.
   b. $4,900.
   c. $2,000.
   d. $13,900.

8. (Same account as in Question 6.) The equity in the customer's account after the liquidation would:
   a. increase by 50 percent of the proceeds.
   b. decrease.
   c. increase by the amount of the sale.
   d. not change.

9. Customer's margin account is as follows:

Market value	$23,200
Debit balance	18,200
Equity	5,000

   The account is on NYSE maintenance call for $800. The customer wishes to deposit marginable securities in the account. What is the minimum amount required?
   a. $1,067.
   b. $1,600.
   c. $3,200.
   d. $800.

10. (Same account as in Question 9.) How long may the broker wait to receive the required funds?
    a. seven business days.
    b. five business days.
    c. fifteen business days.
    d. promptly.

Chapter Four

THE SPECIAL MEMORANDUM ACCOUNT

The special memorandum account, more commonly referred to as the SMA, is unquestionably the most misunderstood account on Wall Street. While the SMA is a separate account as defined by Section 220.6 of Regulation T, it works hand in hand with the customer's margin account. Reprinted below is the section of Regulation T that defines the account and the permissible entries, the wording of which may explain why it is so misunderstood:

> (a) A special memorandum account (SMA) may be maintained in conjunction with a margin account. A single entry amount may be used to represent both a credit to the SMA and a debit to the margin account. A transfer between the two accounts may be effected by an increase or reduction in the entry. When computing the equity in a margin account, the single entry shall be considered as a debit in the margin account. A payment to the customer or on the customer's behalf or a transfer to any of the customer's other accounts from the SMA reduces the single entry amount.
>
> (b) The SMA may contain the following entries:
>
> (1) dividend and interest payments;

(2) cash not required by this part, including cash deposited to meet a maintenance margin call or to meet any requirement of a self-regulatory organization that is not imposed by this part;

(3) proceeds of a sale of securities or cash no longer required on any expired or liquidated security position that may be withdrawn under section 220.4(e) of this part; and

(4) margin excess transferred from the margin account under section 220.4(e)(2) of this part.

The primary purpose of the SMA is to preserve the customer's buying power. As we discussed earlier, buying power is created by having equity in excess of the Regulation T requirement. Here is an example:

Market value	$10,000
Debit balance	4,000
Equity	6,000

Req.	Eq.	
$5,000	$6,000	
	−5,000	
	1,000	excess
	× 2	
	$2,000	buying power

As you can see, this customer has excess equity of $1,000, which may be withdrawn or converted into buying power of $2,000 (customer can purchase $2,000 of securities without depositing any additional funds). However, if the customer did not withdraw the excess funds or purchase additional securities, and the market value of the securities declined to $9,000, the account would look like this:

Market value	$9,000
Debit balance	4,000
Equity	5,000

The Special Memorandum Account

Req.	Eq.	
$5,000	$5,000	
	−4,500	
	500	excess
	× 2	
	$1,000	buying power

By not acting immediately, this customer lost $500 of excess equity thereby reducing his buying power to $1,000. When refiguring a margin account, remember to use the current market value versus the current requirement.

Up until the 1930s, the procedure for preventing a customer from losing buying power was to take the excess out of the customer's margin account and put it into the customer's cash account. This was accomplished by debiting the customer's margin account and crediting the customer's cash account via a journal entry. In addition, an account receivable and an account payable had to be established in the accounting department to reflect the offsetting debit and credit entries. Further complicating this was the adjustment of the customer's debit balance at the end of each month to ensure that the proper interest was charged. This was all done manually and was quite labor intensive.

In the early 1940s, a bright young margin clerk by the name of Aaron Schwaberg read Regulation T and saw a section where a *special miscellaneous account* could be established to meet the needs of the customer. The account was renamed the special memorandum account in 1983 to better describe the entries and actual use of the account.

In any event, the account has long since been referred to as the SMA.

This clerk simply took the customer's margin card (which reflected the customer's holdings, total market value, debit balance and equity) and drew the following on the back of the card (the beginning of the special memorandum account):

SMA

Date	Debit	Credit	Balance	Explanation

This account preserved the customer's buying power, and since it was a memorandum method of accounting, it eliminated a whole bookkeeping record in the accounting department and the accompanying journal entries.

An example of the memorandum method follows:

Customer's Margin Account

Market value	$10,000
Debit balance	4,000
Equity	6,000

Req.	Eq.
$5,000	$6,000
	−5,000
	1,000 excess

The $1,000 is placed in the SMA:

Date	Debit	Credit	Balance	Explanation
12/11/87		$1,000	$1,000	excess over Reg. T

The $1,000 excess is now in a special memorandum account which is a separate and distinct account preserving the customer's buying power of $2,000.

The customer's margin account would still appear the same:

Market value	$10,000
Debit balance	4,000
Equity	6,000

The Special Memorandum Account

There is no increase in the customer's debit balance since the entry to the SMA is a memorandum entry, monies have not left the firm and there has been no additional extension of credit. Consequently, there is no increase in customer's debit balance. If the market value of the customer's securities declines,

Market value	$9,000
Debit balance	4,000
Equity	5,000

the customer would still have buying power of $2,000, since the $1,000 excess was moved to the SMA. In fact, this customer could still withdraw the $1,000 if he so desired. Withdrawals from the SMA are always permitted as long as the withdrawal does not put the account below the NYSE minimum maintenance margin requirements.

Should the customer withdraw the money from the SMA, the SMA would look like this:

Date	Debit	Credit	Balance	Explanation
12/11/87		$1,000	$1,000	excess over Reg. T
12/12/87	$1,000		0	withdrawal

The customer's margin account would now appear as follows:

Market value	$9,000
Debit balance	5,000
Equity	4,000

Notice that the debit balance is now increased by the actual withdrawal because the funds have in fact left the firm, and there was an additional extension of credit. In the event the customer purchased $2,000 of securities instead of withdrawing the funds, the margin account would appear as follows:

Market value	$11,000
Debit balance	6,000
Equity	5,000

The proper entry to the SMA would be:

Date	Debit	Credit	Balance	Explanation
12/11/87		$1,000	$1,000	excess over Reg. T
12/12/87	$1,000		0	pur.100 ABC @20

The SMA is the official record of the customer's account. All entries are permanent and require descriptions informative enough to detail what took place.

Here is a sample of a customer's account giving the proper entries to the customer's margin and SMA accounts, along with detailed explanations.

CUSTOMER'S ACCOUNT

(Long-assume that the following positions were purchased sometime in the past and the required margin deposited.)

Margin Account of John Smith

Long

100	A	24	$2,400
200	B	13	2,600
100	C	10	1,000
200	D	24	4,800

Market value $10,800
Debit balance   3,200
Equity   7,600

Req.	Eq.
$5,400	$7,600
	5,400
	2,200 excess

The Special Memorandum Account

Entry to the SMA

Date	Debit	Credit	Balance	Explanation
1/4/88		$2,200	$2,200	excess over Reg. T

All we have done at this point is determine the customer's total market value and recompute the account to see if there was any excess over the current Regulation T margin requirement of 50 percent. There was, in the amount of $2,200.

The customer now withdraws $1,000.

Date	Debit	Credit	Balance	Explanation
1/4/88		$2,200	$2,200	excess over Reg. T
1/5/88	$1,000		$1,200	withdrawal

Customer's Margin Account

Market value	$10,800
Debit balance	4,200
Equity	6,600

The customer's debit balance was increased and equity decreased to reflect the withdrawal of $1,000.

The customer purchases 100 shares of E @ 50.

Margin Account

100	A	24	$2,400
200	B	13	2,600
100	C	10	1,000
200	D	24	4,800
100	E	50	5,000

Market value	$15,800
Debit balance	9,200
Equity	6,600

As a result of the purchase of 100 E @50 the market value is increased by $5,000, as well as the debit balance. The purchase of 100 E @50 ($5,000) requires 50 percent or $2,500 Reg. T requirement. If we look to the customer's SMA, a portion of the money is there:

Date	Debit	Credit	Balance	Explanation
1/4/88		$2,200	$2,200	excess over Reg. T
1/5/88	$1,000		$1,200	withdrawal
1/6/88	1,200		0	buy 100 E @50, T call $1,300

There was a requirement for $2,500, and $1,200 was available in the customer's SMA. The $1,200 was subtracted from the balance in the SMA (applied to the T call), and $1,200 was subtracted from the requirement (supplied from the SMA). A Regulation T call was issued for $1,300. Note that the Balance column in the SMA can only be a credit balance or a zero balance—never a debit balance.

Market value	$15,800
Debit balance	7,900
Equity	7,900

The debit balance is reduced by the amount of the deposit. However, there is no entry to the customer's SMA. This is because the money in the SMA was used to meet the Regulation T call.

Dividends of $1,000 per share are declared on the holdings of 100 A, 200 B, and 100 C.

The effect on the margin account is this:

Market value	$15,800
Debit balance	7,500
Equity	8,300

The Special Memorandum Account

The money received ($400) would reduce the customer's debit balance. Again, anytime money is received into the account the debit balance is reduced. Now, since the monies received were not required by Regulation T, they may be placed into the customer's SMA.

Date	Debit	Credit	Balance	Explanation
1/4/88		$2,200	$2,200	excess over Reg. T
1/5/88	$1,000		$1,200	withdrawal
1/6/88	1,200		0	buy 100 E @50, T call $1,300
1/7/88		400	400	div. $1.00 on 100 A, 200 B, 100 C

Now let's assume the market value of the securities decline as follows:

100	A	20	$2,000
200	B	10	2,000
100	C	6	600
200	D	19	3,800
100	E	37	3,700

Market value	$12,100
Debit balance	7,500
Equity	4,600

Anytime there is a sharp decline in the market value of securities, the margin account should be checked to see how the account stands as far as meeting the NYSE minimum maintenance requirement of 25 percent.

	Req.	Eq.	
	$5,400	$4,600	
		3,025	
		$1,575	excess over NYSE min. maint. req.

The customer wishes to withdraw $200. (This is a permissible withdrawal because the customer's margin account would still be above NYSE maintenance after the withdrawal.)

The margin account after the withdrawal:

Market value	$12,100
Debit balance	7,700
Equity	4,400

The entry to the SMA:

Date	Debit	Credit	Balance	Explanation
1/4/88		$2,200	$2,200	excess over Reg. T
1/5/88	$1,000		$1,200	withdrawal
1/6/88	1,200		0	buy 100 E @50, T call $1,300
1/7/88		400	400	div. $1.00 on 100 A, 200 B, 100 C
1/8/88	200		200	withdrawal

The customer sells 200 B @10. After the sale of securities the account will appear as follows:

100	A	20	$2,000
100	C	6	600
200	D	19	3,800
100	E	37	3,700

Market value	$10,100
Debit balance	5,700
Equity	4,400

The Special Memorandum Account

Sales of securities will release funds in the amount of 50 percent of the sale proceeds.

Entry to the SMA:

Date	Debit	Credit	Balance	Explanation
1/4/88		$2,200	$2,200	excess over Reg. T
1/5/88	$1,000		$1,200	withdrawal
1/6/88	1,200		0	buy 100 E @50, T call $1,300
1/7/88		400	400	div. $1.00 on 100 A, 200 B, 100 C
1/8/88	200		200	withdrawal
1/11/88		1,000	1,200	sale of 200 B @10

Customer now withdraws $1,200 cash.

Entry to SMA:

Date	Debit	Credit	Balance	Explanation
1/4/88		$2,200	$2,200	excess over Reg. T
1/5/88	$1,000		$1,200	withdrawal
1/6/88	1,200		0	buy 100 E @50, T call $1,300
1/7/88		400	400	div. $1.00 on 100 A, 200 B, 100 C
1/8/88	200		200	withdrawal
1/11/88		1,000	1,200	sale of 200 B @10
1/12/88	1,200		0	withdrawal

Customer's margin account after the withdrawal:

Market value	$10,100
Debit balance	6,900
Equity	3,200

Customer sells 100 A @ 20:

100	C	6	$ 600
200	D	19	3,800
100	E	37	3,700

Market value	$8,100
Debit balance	4,900
Equity	3,200

Entry to SMA:

Date	Debit	Credit	Balance	Explanation
1/4/88		$2,200	$2,200	excess over Reg. T
1/5/88	$1,000		$1,200	withdrawal
1/6/88	1,200		0	buy 100 E @50, T call $1,300
1/7/88		400	400	div. $1.00 on 100 A, 200 B, 100 C
1/8/88	200		200	withdrawal
1/11/88		1,000	1,200	sale of 200 B @10
1/12/88	1,200		0	withdrawal
1/13/88		1,000	1,000	sale of 100 A @20

The Special Memorandum Account

The market value of D drops to 9 per share.

100	C	6	$ 600
200	D	9	1,800
100	E	37	3,700

Market value	$6,100
Debit balance	4,900
Equity	1,200

In light of the market decline, let us examine how this affects the account from the standpoint of NYSE minimum maintenance requirements.

	Req.	*Eq.*
	$1,525	$1,200
	−1,200	
NYSE call	$ 325	

This account is on stock exchange maintenance margin call for $325. In our example, we will request the $325, and assume that *customer deposits the requested amount*. The customer's margin account will reflect this as follows:

Market value	$6,100
Debit balance	4,575
Equity	1,525

Money came into the account, thereby reducing the debit balance by the amount of the deposit ($325). Additionally, since the funds were not required by Regulation T, they may be credited to the customer's SMA by the amount of the deposit.

The customer's SMA:

Date	Debit	Credit	Balance	Explanation
1/4/88		$2,200	$2,200	excess over Reg. T
1/5/88	$1,000		$1,200	withdrawal
1/6/88	1,200		0	buy 100 E @50, T call $1,300
1/7/88		400	400	div. $1.00 on 100 A, 200 B, 100 C
1/8/88	200		200	withdrawal
1/11/88		1,000	1,200	sale of 200 B @10
1/12/88	1,200		0	withdrawal
1/13/88		1,000	1,000	sale of 100 A @20
1/14/88		325	1,325	deposit of funds

As you can see, the balance in the customer's SMA is $1,325; however the customer may not withdraw any of these funds, as a withdrawal would put the account below NYSE minimum maintenance requirements. At the same time, the balance would not be eliminated, for if the market rises, the customer could use part or all of these funds depending on the increase in the account's market value.

Market value of the securities increase:

100	C	25	$2,500
200	D	15	3,000
100	E	40	4,000

The Special Memorandum Account

Market value	$9,500
Debit balance	4,575
Equity	4,925

There appears to be excess over Regulation T, therefore the account should be recomputed:

Req.	Eq.
$4,750	$4,925
	−4,750
	175 excess over Reg. T

The $175 excess over Regulation T may not be credited to the SMA because the excess is less than the current balance of the SMA ($175 excess over Reg. T versus $1,325 balance in SMA). However, in the event Reg. T excess exceeds the current balance in the SMA the difference may be made up in the SMA. For example, if the excess over Regulation T came to $1,600, $275 could be credited to the SMA to bring it from $1,325 to $1,600. In our example this is not the case, so no entry is made to the SMA.

The customer purchases 100 F @50.

100	C	25	$2,500
200	D	15	3,000
100	E	40	4,000
100	F	50	5,000

Market Value	$14,500
Debit Balance	9,575
Equity	4,925

The $5,000 purchase requires 50 percent or $2,500. The customer's SMA has $1,325.

Required	$2,500
SMA	−1,325
Reg. T call	1,175

58   Chapter 4

Date	Debit	Credit	Balance	Explanation
1/4/88		$2,200	$2,200	excess over Reg. T
1/5/88	$1,000		$1,200	withdrawal
1/6/88	1,200		0	buy 100 E @50, T call $1,300
1/7/88		400	400	div. $1.00 on 100 A, 200 B, 100 C
1/8/88	200		200	withdrawal
1/11/88		1,000	1,200	sale of 200 B @10
1/12/88	1,200		0	withdrawal
1/13/88		1,000	1,000	sale of 100 A @20
1/14/88		325	1,325	deposit of funds
1/15/88	1,325		0	buy 100 F @50, T call $1,175

After the deposit of funds to meet the Regulation T call the account now appears:

        Market value $14,500
        Debit balance   8,400
        Equity   6,100

No entry to the customer's SMA is made because the funds deposited were required by Regulation T. Only the customer's debit balance was reduced. Also note that the customer's margin

The Special Memorandum Account

account is still classified as restricted, just as it was for a good portion of the month. Yet this in no way restricted the customer's ability to trade.

CHAPTER FOUR QUESTIONS

1. The SMA is used to:
   a. satisfy NYSE calls.
   b. satisfy so-called house calls.
   c. purchase securities.
   d. preserve the customer's buying power.

2. A withdrawal of funds from the SMA will always:
   a. increase the customer's debit balance.
   b. increase the customer's equity.
   c. be permitted.
   d. increase the market value of securities held in the customer's margin account.

3. Cash deposited to meet an outstanding Regulation T call will:
   a. increase the debit balance.
   b. not affect the SMA.
   c. decrease the equity in the account.
   d. increase the market value of securities.

4. Fully paid for listed securities deposited in a customer's margin account, the customer may credit the customer's SMA:
   a. zero.
   b. 100 percent of the current market value of the securities.
   c. 50 percent of the current market value of the securities.
   d. 25 percent of the current market value of the securities.

5. Monies in the SMA may be withdrawn:
   a. only if after the withdrawal the margin account would not be restricted.
   b. to purchase securities only.
   c. in amounts of $2,000 or more.
   d. provided the account was above NYSE minimum maintenance requirements after withdrawal.

6. As a result of increasing interest rates, a customer reduces his debit balance by depositing $10,000 into his margin account. The proper entry to his SMA would be:
   a. credit SMA $10,000.
   b. to reduce his debit balance.
   c. no entry to the SMA.
   d. none of the above.

7. A customer is on NYSE maintenance call for $750. The customer sends a check for $750, the proper entry to the SMA would be:
   a. no entry to the SMA.
   b. credit the account $750.
   c. credit the account $1,500.
   d. debit the account $750.

8. A customer's margin account is on NYSE maintenance call for $1,000. The customer also has a balance of $5,000 in his SMA and instructs his broker to take the $1,000 out of his SMA to meet the maintenance call. The proper entry to the SMA would be:
   a. debit the account $1,000.
   b. credit the account $1,000.
   c. no entry to the SMA; improper request.
   d. credit margin account, debit SMA.

9. Dividend received on a holding in the margin account may:
   a. be credited to the SMA.
   b. be debited to the SMA.
   c. increase the debit balance.
   d. decrease the customer's equity.

10. A customer's margin account has excess over Regulation T of $1,500 and a credit balance of $1,700 in his SMA, you would be permitted to:
    a. increase SMA by $200.
    b. decrease SMA by $200.
    c. credit SMA 50 percent or $1,500.
    d. do nothing.

Chapter Five

SHORT SALES

Prior to describing the actual mechanics of short selling, a little background information may be helpful. Up to this point, we have been describing purchases on margin that create a *long* position. If you own securities, you are considered long. When you sell these securities, it is a *long sale*.

As you know, the vast majority of investors look for a corporation that has a good product or product line, look into the management (is it efficient? innovative? aggressive?), check the competition, and look at the price. If they believe the security is undervalued, investors will buy with the expectation that the price will increase, resulting in a profit.

The short seller investigates in the same way but is looking for an outdated product, poor management, and strong competition. This investor feels the security is overvalued. Consequently, this investor will sell the security with the intention of buying it back some time in the future at a cheaper price, again resulting in a profit.

A short sale is defined by the Securities Exchange Act of 1934 as the sale of a security not owned by the investor, or if owned, the investor does not intend to deliver. In most business transactions, if you sell something you don't own, you probably will go to jail for fraud. In the securities industry it is done all the time. Fraud is avoided by borrowing securities and delivering the borrowed securities to the buyer.

To have any transaction, there must be a buyer and a seller; the same applies with short sales. However, this transaction differs slightly in that a third party is involved, a *lender*.

The lender is usually an institution or broker-dealer but may be an individual who has a large, well-diversified portfolio and is willing to lend the securities.

One of the requirements to sell short is that you must be in a position to borrow the securities. The short seller borrows the securities and in turn sells them to the buyer. When he delivers the securities to the buyer he receives payment.

```
Lender                    Short Seller                Buyer
   ◄─────────────────────── $10,000  ◄───────────────────
100 ABC ──────────────────────────────────────────► 100 ABC
```

At this point one wonders, "Why would the owner of the securities lend them to the short seller in the first place?" The lender is going to receive as collateral 100 percent of the market value (or the proceeds) of the short sale.

```
        Short Seller          Buyer
        – 100 ABC            100 ABC

        Lender          ┐
        $10,000      ◄──┘
```

We now have a buyer who purchased the securities and paid for them. For him, this transaction is over. We still have a short seller who owes 100 shares of ABC to the lender, and a lender who is holding $10,000 in cash as collateral for the stock loan, which can be reinvested in short-term, interest-producing money-market instruments.

```
        Short Seller          Lender
        – 100 ABC            + $10,000
```

Short Sales

This is what makes the stock loan business so profitable. Remember, the lender is still the owner of the security. He did not sell or give it to the short seller—he lent it. As the owner of the security, he is entitled to all dividends and distributions such as rights offerings and spinoffs and also market appreciation.

As a result of this short sale, we have created two 100 ABC long positions; one is the buyer, the other the lender. Therefore, any distribution by the company must be met by the short seller to the lender. If a $100 dividend is declared, when it is payable, the short seller pays the lender. If a rights offering is made, the short seller must purchase the rights in the open market and deliver the rights to the lender. If there is a stock split, the short seller now owes the lender 200 shares. As you see, the lender is still very much the owner of the security. The only privilege that the lender may lose is the right to vote (a small consideration compared to the benefits).

The lender has converted his portfolio from stock certificates to cash and still retained ownership. As a result of having this excess cash, the lender will invest it in some money market instrument such as a Treasury bill, certificates of deposit, bankers' acceptance, or commercial paper. Therefore, the lender has enhanced his net worth by whatever interest is earned on the money market instruments. In addition, the lender is completely protected. He has 100 percent of the market value, and, should the short seller disappear, the lender has sufficient money to repurchase the stock and go back to his original position.

In order to protect the lender as well as the short seller, the brokerage firm goes through a procedure known as *mark to the market* to ensure that the lender will have 100 percent of the current market value of the securities regardless of market fluctuations. Our example looks like this:

Short Seller	*Lender*
– 100 ABC	+ $10,000

If the market value of 100 ABC increased to $12,000, the lender would no longer have 100 percent of the market value of the securities. So the brokerage firm would take $2,000 from the short seller's account and give it to the lender to boost the collateral to its proper level. This is accomplished by debiting the short seller $2,000 and crediting the lender $2,000. After the mark to the market is complete, our example now looks this way:

Short Seller
– 100 ABC
$2,000 debit

Lender
+ $12,000

Now suppose the reverse happens and the market value declines to $9,000. The lender is holding $12,000, and the securities borrowed are worth only $9,000. The lender has too much. Therefore a *reverse mark to the market* is made, crediting the short seller's account and debiting the lender's account. Again, the lender is entitled to only 100 percent of the market value. Our example, after this:

Short Seller
– 100 ABC
$1,000 credit

Lender
+ $9,000

As a result of crediting the short seller with $3,000, the $2,000 debit balance was eliminated and, in fact, a credit balance was created. The lender's credit was reduced to $9,000.

To close out his position, the short seller must return 100 ABC to the lender. He might buy the shares in the open market for $9,000 and return them. Once the 100 ABC is returned, the lender must return the collateral—in this case $9,000. In fact, the $9,000 collateral that the lender surrenders is used to pay for the purchase of the 100 ABC.

Short Seller
$1,000 credit
Seller of the 100 ABC
$9,000

Lender
100 ABC

The short seller has repaid the stock loan, the lender has the 100 ABC, the seller of the securities has been paid, and there is a $1,000 credit balance in the short seller's account, representing his profit.

In the event the short seller closed the position out at $12,000, a $2,000 debit would exist in the account representing his loss.

There are several additional important points regarding short sales. As previously stated, a prerequisite to selling short is the ability to borrow the securities. Most firms have a department called the stock loan department that arranges for the loans either within or outside the firm.

When a short sale is entered into, the order must be marked as "short." All sell orders are identified as long (you are the owner) or short (you are selling borrowed securities).

Additionally, if a customer is selling a security short, and if that security is traded on a national securities exchange, the customer is subject to what is known as the *up-tick requirement*. This requirement is found in the Securities Exchange Act of 1934.

Sales of securities have a bearish effect on the market. More sells than buys drive the price of securities down. More buys than sells drive the price of securities up. Prior to the Securities Exchange Act of 1934, when bad news came out on a particular company, a customer would sell that security short, further depressing the market. This abuse was ended by the up-tick requirement.

For example, if the security opened for trading, and trades occurred as follows: 20, 19 ⅞, 19 ¾, 19 ⅝, 19 ¾, 19 ¾, 19 ⅝, the opening sale is 20 followed by the next sale of 19 ⅞. This is known as a *down* or *minus tick* because it is lower than the sale before it, and you may *not* sell short at this price. The next sale, 19 ¾, is again a minus tick, and again no short sale is permitted; the same applies to 19 ⅝.

At 19 ¾, a short sale may be made, since this sale is higher than the previous one. This is an example of an *up* or *plus tick*. The up tick is only from the previous sale of the stock and does not have to be up for the day. The next sale, 19 ¾, is known as a zero-plus tick because it is the same as the last sale but higher than the last different price, and a short sale may be executed. Short sales can be made only on the plus or zero-plus tick.

Although the order is marked short, and the short seller is subject to the up-tick requirement, the other side of the transaction (either listed or over-the-counter) neither knows nor cares that the seller is short. The buyer will receive the stock and must pay for it. On the floor of the exchanges, the last sales price is indicated with a 19 ¾+ or 19 ⅝– at the post where the security is traded, so the broker executing the short sale knows if it is a plus or minus tick and can place his order in compliance with the up-tick requirement.

Thus far, we have examined the mechanics of the short sale. What does this look like in the customer's margin account? Years ago, when posting was done manually, margin clerks always separated long positions from short positions by keeping all of the long positions on one side of the card and all short positions on the other, making it easy to distinguish one from the other.

Along came the computer and made it necessary to separate long and short positions by placing them in separate records. Thus, you hear the term *short account*. Though it may sound like a different account, the short account is simply a part of the customer's margin account.

In fact, Regulation T requires all short sales to be made in the margin account. Using the same short sale transaction described previously, we will see how this transaction is handled in the customer's margin account.

Customer sells short 100 ABC for $10,000.

Customer's Margin Account

Short Account
$10,000 SMV
$10,000 credit

T-call for $5,000.

The short sale is placed in the customer's short account. As in purchases, the customer is required to deposit 50 percent of the short market value in accordance with Regulation T. The same time restrictions apply (deposit promptly—five business days, must be received in seven business days). Assume the customer deposits the required amount ($5,000). Our customer's margin account after the deposit appears:

Margin Account
$5,000 credit

Short Account
$10,000 SMV
10,000 credit

Notice that the $5,000 credit was placed in the customer's margin account and not in the short account. If the customer had a debit balance, the debit would have to be reduced by the amount of the deposit. The SMV (short market value) is $10,000. However, the credit balance under the SMV is known as a *ledger credit balance*. That credit balance represents the proceeds of the short sale that is not in the customer's account but rather is securing the stock loan, enabling the customer to make the short sale and then deliver the borrowed shares.

As the market value increased to $12,000, here is what the account would look like:

Margin Account   *Short Account*
$5,000 credit $12,000 SMV
                          10,000 credit

Looking at the credit in the short account, it is clear that the lender does not have the full market value of the shares being lent. Now we must mark the transaction to the market. We would take $2,000 from the short seller and send it to the lender. Afterwards, the account would look like this:

Margin Account   *Short Account*
$3,000 credit $12,000 SMV
                          12,000 credit

You can see that the lender now has 100 percent of the market value, and the credit in the customer's margin account was reduced by the amount of the mark to the market.

Next, we indicated that the market value declined to $9,000 (the short seller was correct—the market value of the securities went down). The short seller's account would now appear:

Margin Account   *Short Account*
$3,000 credit $ 9,000 SMV
                          12,000 credit

Again, it is clear the market value of the sold securities is now $9,000, but the lender is holding $12,000 as collateral. Now we will perform a reverse mark to the market. The lender will send the short seller $3,000 and our account would look this:

Margin Account
$6,000 credit

Short Account
$9,000 SMV
9,000 credit

This account as it stands, has $1,500 excess over Regulation T and $3,000 Buying Power.

Req.	*Eg.*	
$4,500	$6,000	
	− 4,500	
	1,500	excess
	× 2	
	$3,000	buying power or short selling power

The same principle of recomputing the Regulation T requirement applies to the account on the short side as on the long side: 50 percent of the current market value, whether it is long market value or short market value.

The equity in this short account is calculated by subtracting the short market value from the credit balance ($9,000 − $9,000 = 0). However, long and short accounts *must be combined* when recomputing the margin account. In our example there is no long market value and no debit balance in the margin account, just a credit balance of $6,000. This is the equity.

The excess of $1,500 may also be placed in the customer's SMA for future use. Let's assume that the customer wishes to buy $3,000 of listed securities in the margin account. After the purchase, the account would appear as follows:

Margin Account
MV $3,000
Credit 3,000
Equity 6,000

Short Account
SMV $9,000
Credit 9,000

Notice that the credit balance in the long account decreased by the full amount of the purchase, yet the equity remained the same.

Short Sales

All we did was change the composition of the equity. Instead of all cash, the equity is now a mixture of cash and securities. Recomputation of the account now will show the account is right at the 50 percent level.

Req.	Eq.
$1,500	$6,000
4,500	0
6,000	6,000

Fifty percent of the long market value is $1,500; equity in the account is $6,000; 50 percent of the short market value is $4,500; and equity on the short side is zero. Equity on the short side will always be zero, because the short market value and the credit balance are marked to the market on a daily basis.

COVERING OF SHORT SALES

The term *covering a short sale* simply means a customer closes out the short position by purchasing the securities that were sold short and returning them to the lender. (Short sales may also be covered by delivering a long position to the lender. This procedure will be discussed later.)

How does our account now stand?

Margin Account				Short Account			
100	A	@10	$1,000	100	X	@40	4,000
100	B	@12	1,200	100	Y	@50	5,000
100	C	@ 8	800				

Market value	$3,000	Short market value	$9,000
Credit balance	3,000	Credit balance	9,000
Equity	6,000		

The customer wishes to close out the short position of 100 Y @50. The customer would enter a buy order for 100 Y. When purchased, it will be delivered to the lender to repay the stock borrowed. The effect on the customer's account is as follows:

Margin Account					Short Account			
100	A	@10	$1,000		100	X	@40	$4,000
100	B	@12	1,200					
100	C	@ 8	800					

Market value $3,000   Short market value $4,000
Credit balance   3,000   Credit balance   4,000
Equity   6,000

SMA

Date	Debit	Credit	Balance	Explanation
1/5/88		$2,500		Pur. 100 y to cover short

Covering a short position reduces the short market value as well as the credit balance. The credit balance is reduced because we have returned the stock to the lender. Consequently, the lender had to return the collateral ($5,000). In fact, we used that $5,000 to purchase the 100 Y. The credit to the customer's SMA represents the permissible release on the covering of a short sale, 50 percent of the cost. Hence, cost of cover was $5,000, and 50 percent of this is $2,500—the amount credited to the SMA.

To summarize briefly, short sales of securities are subject to Regulation T just as are long purchases: 50 percent of short sale proceeds must be deposited into the customer's account "promptly"—no later than seven business days.

NYSE MINIMUM MAINTENANCE REQUIREMENTS

Just as on the long side, the short side has minimum maintenance requirements as well. However, they are a little more complex. As previously stated, a short sale is a risky position, as one could suffer

Short Sales

unlimited losses. Consequently, the NYSE established higher requirements on low-priced securities. This is because the chance of a security selling at $60 or $70 per share doubling in a short period of time is relatively small compared to the chance of a security selling at $2 or $3 doing so. Therefore, Rule 431 of the NYSE requires the following minimum maintenance for short sales:

1. $2.50 per share or 100 percent of the market value, whichever amount is greater for each stock selling below $5.00 per share.
2. $5.00 per share or 30 percent of the market value, whichever amount is greater for each stock selling at $5.00 and above.

The requirements sound worse than they really are. For example, for 100 shares of XYZ selling at $3.00 per share, the requirement is:

$2.50 per share $2.50 × 100 shares = $250
                    or
100% of the market value $3.00 × 100 shares = $300,

whichever is greater. $300 is more than $250, so $300 is the requirement.

Another example: for 100 XYZ @10 ($1,000), the requirement is:

$5.00 per share $5.00 × 100 shares = $500
                    or
30% of the market value 30% × $1000 = $300

whichever is greater. Therefore, $500 is the requirement.

The break point actually comes at 16 ¾, since: 30% of 16 ¾ = $5.02, which is greater than $5.00 a share. Therefore, anytime you see a security selling above 16 ¾, the minimum maintenance requirement is a straight 30 percent of the market value. However, if the price is below 16 ¾, the special requirements for lower priced stocks come into effect.

SAMPLE TRANSACTIONS

A customer's account contains the following long and short positions, and we want to determine the condition of the account with respect to the NYSE minimum maintenance requirements.

Long Margin Account					Short Account			
100	A	@35	$3,500	100	X	@40	$2,000
100	B	@16	1,600	200	Y	@10	2,000
200	C	@22	4,400	100	Z	@ 2	200
100	D	@ 8	800				

Market value	$10,300	Short market value	$4,200
Debit balance	6,500	Credit balance	4,200
Equity	3,800		

```
                          Req.              Eq.
                         $2,575           $3,800
                            600                0
                          1,000            3,800   total equity
                            250
Total requirement         4,425
less total equity        -3,800
NYSE call                   625
```

The above account is on NYSE minimum maintenance call for $625. We arrived at this figure through the following steps.

Step 1. The long market value is $10,300. The minimum maintenance requirement on the long side is 25 percent of the current market value, which is the first figure under the Req. column in the example ($2,575).

Step 2. When figuring the requirements on the short side, each security must be looked at separately if any is selling at less than 16 3/4. In the event all the securities were selling at 16 3/4 or above, just take 30 percent of the total short market value.

Step 3. However, neither is the case in our example. The first security short is 100 X @20. The requirement is 30 percent of the market value ($600) or $5.00 per share ($500), whichever is greater.

Short Sales

The greater of the two ($600) is the requirement (shown as the second figure under the Req. column in our example). The next security short is 200 Y @10 per share. This requirement is again $5.00 per share ($1,000) or 30 percent of the market value ($600), whichever is greater. $1,000 is the requirement (shown as the third figure under the Req. column). The last security short is 100 Z @2. The requirement for this security is $2.50 per share ($250) or 100 percent of the market value ($200), again, whichever is greatest. Two hundred and fifty dollars is the minimum maintenance requirement for this security (fourth figure under the Req. column).

Step 4. Total requirement is the sum of all the requirements, both long and short. In the event the equity exceeded the requirement, there would have been excess over NYSE minimum maintenance requirements. However, this was not the case. The requirements exceeded the equity and the difference, $625, is the minimum NYSE maintenance call.

Notice the requirement on the 100 Z sold short @2 exceeds the cost of covering the security. Recall that on the long side, a broker would never ask a customer for more than the full cost of the security. But a short position always has a higher degree of exposure. Consequently, requirements for short sales often exceed the market value of the security sold short.

Remember we indicated that there were four ways to meet a margin call:

1. Deposit the required funds.
2. Liquidation.
3. Depositing additional collateral.
4. Market appreciation.

The same four ways apply to the short side. However, meeting a margin call by liquidation on the short side is accomplished by purchasing the same security (buying in). There is one other difference. On the long side, meeting a margin call by liquidation requires selling securities with a value of four times the amount of the maintenance call. However, in this example covering or buying in 200 shares of Y @10 would eliminate a dollar requirement of

$1,000, bringing the account back into compliance with the NYSE maintenance requirement and, in fact, giving the account some excess over the minimum requirement.

	Long Margin Account				Short Account		
100	A	@35	$3,500	100	X	@20	$2,000
100	B	@16	1,600	100	Z	@ 2	200
200	C	@22	4,400				
100	D	@ 8	800				

Market value	$10,300	Short market value	$2,200
Debit balance	6,500	Credit balance	2,200
Equity	3,800		

```
         Req.           Eq.
        $2,575         $3,800
           600              0
           250          3,800   total equity
         3,425         -3,425
                          375   excess over NYSE
                                maint. requirement
```

SMA

Date	Debit	Credit	Balance	Explanation
1/7/88		$1,000	$1,000	cover 200 Y @20

SHORT SALE VERSUS THE BOX OR SHORT AGAINST THE BOX

Let us go back to the original definition of a short sale, found in the Securities Exchange Act of 1934: "…the sale of a security that you do not own or if you own it you do not intend to deliver it." Thus far, we have discussed only short sales where the customer does not own the security and is required to borrow it to complete the sale.

Short Sales

The term *short against the box* is a short sale where the customer owns the security and wishes to sell the same security short. First of all, why would someone wish to sell a security short when they own it? Why not just sell it long? The primary reason is for tax purposes. A customer may have purchased a security that has since appreciated substantially. However, if the customer sells the security now, income tax must be paid on the profit in the current tax year, a year in which he has a substantial income. He anticipates his income will be lower next year, since he is planning to retire. If the sale could be made next year, this would result in a lower tax being paid on the profit. However, if he waits, he runs the risk that the market price of the security will decline, wiping out any profits. It would be in a case such as this that a customer would execute a short sale against the box.

A short sale against the box is handled exactly as a straight short sale as far as execution and operation; i.e., the customer must be in position to borrow the security he is selling. (The IRS has ruled that if a customer uses the long position to deliver versus the short, the position is considered closed out.) Further, the order must be marked as a short sale and the up-tick requirement is in force if the security is trading on a national securities exchange.

Back to our customer who wants to sell short versus the box (the term means the long security owned by the customer is in the possession of the broker). Since marginal securities are financed, a portion of the customer's securities will be kept in the "active box," as opposed to segregation (for fully paid for securities) where the securities are locked up for safekeeping. (A more detailed explanation of segregation will follow later on.)

When the short sale takes place, the customer will be both long 100 shares of A stock and short 100 shares of A stock, as a result of using borrowed shares for the delivery.

The customer's margin account prior to the short sale was:

Margin Account

Long

100	A	40	$4,000
100	B	25	2,500

200	C	30	6,000
100	D	15	1,500

Market value	$14,000
Debit balance	8,000
Equity	6,000

No SMA balance.

Notice that this account is restricted, since the equity ($6,000) is below the current margin requirement ($7,000). After the short sale against the box, the account now appears:

Margin Long Account

100	A	@40	$4,000
100	B	@25	2,500
200	C	@30	6,000
100	D	@15	1,500

Market value	$14,000
Debit balance	8,000
Equity	6,000

Short Account

100	A	40	$4,000

Short market value	$4,000
Credit balance	4,000

SMA

Date	Debit	Credit	Balance	Explanation
12/2/87		$2,000	$2,000	short versus box 100 A

Notice that the long market value, debit balance, and equity remain unchanged. This is because the customer is still long 100 A @40. Money did not come into or go out of the account.

In the short account is the new position short 100 A @40. The proceeds of the short sale, which is being held as collateral by the lender of the securities, becomes the credit balance. The customer's SMA started off with zero and now has a credit balance of $2,000 or buying power of $4,000. Under Regulation T, if a customer is both long and short in the same security, the account is flat—i.e., the net

Short Sales

position is zero. Regulation T requires no margin and allows for the release of 50 percent of the sale proceeds ($2,000) to the SMA. However, there is a NYSE minimum maintenance requirement of 5 percent of the long side, and an obligation to mark the short side to the market.

Watch what happens if the market value of the securities in the account increases as follows:

Margin Long Account				Short Account			
100	A	50	$5,000	100	A	50	$5,000
100	B	30	3,000				
200	C	40	8,000				
100	D	20	2,000				

Market value	$18,000	Short market value	$5,000
Debit balance	8,000	Credit balance	4,000
Equity	10,000		

Remember, the customer is actually short and there is a lender of securities that is holding only $4,000 as collateral when the securities are actually worth $5,000. Therefore, there must be a mark to the market of $1,000. We will increase the customer debit balance by $1,000 and increase the customer's credit balance by $1,000 to reflect how much the lender is actually holding. After the mark to the market the account appears as follows:

Market value	$18,000	Short market value	$5,000
Debit balance	9,000	Credit balance	5,000
Equity	9,000		

Let's recompute the account for Regulation T purposes to see if there is any additional excess or buying power.

Req.	Eq.	
$6,500	$9,000	
	−6,500	
	2,500	excess over Reg. T

SMA

Date	Debit	Credit	Balance	Explanation
12/2/87		$2,000	$2,000	short versus box 100 A
12/8/87		500	2,500	excess over Reg. T

The excess is $2,500; however, the SMA can only be credited an additional $500, bringing the balance up $2,500. Also note that the requirement is only $6,500, which represents 50 percent of the market value of 100 B, 200 C, and 100 D ($13,000). There is no Regulation T requirement on the 100 A @50. There is a NYSE minimum maintenance requirement of 5 percent of the market value of A, and the short side must be kept marked to the market. This is why we increased the customer's debit balance and credit balance each by $1,000.

Refiguring this account for NYSE purposes, the following takes place:

Req.	Eg.	
250	$9,000	
3,250	−3,500	
3,500	5,500	excess over NYSE minimum maintenance requirement

The $250 requirement represents the 5 percent maintenance on the long side of the short against the box position in A and the $3,250 is the normal 25 percent of the market value of the remaining long securities ($13,000).

On January 12, 1988, the customer decides to close out his borrowed securities by delivering the 100 shares of A that were held in his long margin account to the lender. The margin account would appear as follows:

Margin Long Account
100   B   30 $3,000
200   C   40   8,000
100   D   20   2,000

Short Account
0   0

Short Sales

Market value	$13,000
Debit balance	3,000
Equity	10,000

The market value is reduced by $5,000, since the long position was taken out and delivered to the lender of the securities. In addition, the debit balance is also reduced by $5,000, which was the collateral that the lender was holding for the stock loan. When, the securities were returned, so was the collateral. The short account is zero since the position was closed out.

The closing of the short against the box does not cause an entry to the customer's SMA, because the release was put into the SMA at the time the short against the box was originally made. However, as a result of closing out the short against the box, there appears to be excess over Regulation T. Since virtually all margin accounts are now computerized, the account would automatically be refigured for Regulation T excess.

Req.	Eq.	
$6,500	$10,000	
	− 6,500	
	3,500	excess
	− 2,500	previous SMA
	1,000	additional credit to the customer's SMA

The excess is $3,500, but the previous balance was $2,500. Therefore, we now credit only $1,000 additional.

The point of the whole transaction was to lock in the profit in the security and to insulate the customer from any price fluctuations. The IRS has ruled that the date the long position was delivered to close out the borrowed securities is the date the securities were sold. In our example, this is January 12, 1988. Consequently, the customer has avoided paying the expected higher tax rate since he closed the position in 1988 instead of 1987.

CHAPTER FIVE QUESTIONS

1. Before securities can be sold short, which of the following are required?
    a. The broker must be in a position to borrow the securities.
    b. The order must be marked short.
    c. If listed you are subject to the up-tick requirement.
    d. All of the above

2. The NYSE minimum maintenance requirement on a short position 1,000 shares of ABC @$1.00 is:
    a. $500.
    b. $2,500.
    c. $250.
    d. $1,000.

3. A short sale against the box of $10,000 requires how much for Regulation T?
    a. $5,000.
    b. $2,500.
    c. $1,000.
    d. 0.

4. The covering of a short sale for $7,500 will release how much to the customer's SMA?
    a. $3,750.
    b. No release on the covering of a short.
    c. $2,250.
    d. $7,500.

5. The NYSE minimum maintenance requirement on a short position of 100 ABC @50 is:
    a. $2,500.
    b. $1,500.
    c. $1,250.
    d. $5,000.

Short Sales

6. Customer has a short market of $35,000 and a total credit balance of $60,000. The equity in this account is:
   a. $25,000.
   b. $85,000.
   c. $30,000.
   d. $60,000.

7. (Same account as in Question 6.) This account would be classified as a:
   a. short account.
   b. cash account.
   c. margin account.
   d. restricted margin account.

8. Which of the following choices shows a 0+ tick?
   a. 36 1/2, 36 1/2, 36 3/8, 36 1/2.
   b. 36 1/2, 36 3/8, 36 3/4, 36 3/8.
   c. 36 1/2, 36 5/8, 36 5/8, 36 1/2.
   d. 36 1/2, 36 3/8, 36 1/4, 36 3/8.

9. An initial transaction in a customer's margin account is a short sale of 100 XYZ @5. The required deposit is:
   a. $250.
   b. $2,000.
   c. $500.
   d. $1,000.

10. A customer is short 100 ABC and a 3 for 2 stock split is declared by ABC company. The customer is now short how many shares?
    a. 200 shares
    b. 100 shares
    c. 150 shares
    d. 50 shares

Chapter Six

BONDS

Bonds are a vital part of the securities industry and, in total, constitute a far larger market than stocks, which get all the attention. The news media always refer to the Dow Jones averages and trading volume on the New York Stock Exchange, but the dollar volume of bond trading dwarfs the value of stock trading. We will discuss only a few of the many types of bonds issued today, since our focus is on bonds in the margin account. Categories as far as margin trading is concerned are:

Listed convertible bonds.
Listed debt securities.
OTC margin debt securities.
Exempted securities.
U.S. government obligations and political subdivisions of the United States (states, counties, cities, etc.) more commonly referred to as municipals or munis.
Certain foreign sovereign debt securities.

Prior to getting into the nuts and bolts of trading bonds in the margin account, some background information may be helpful. Earlier we explained that, when the equity in a margin account falls below the existing margin requirement, the account becomes restricted and is subject to the 50 percent retention requirement. The effect of this retention requirement was to limit the amount of money that could be withdrawn on sales of securities in a restricted margin account. When the retention requirement went into effect the initial margin requirement was 90 percent. For example, the customer's account is as follows:

Market value	$10,000
Debit balance	3,000
Equity	7,000

Since the equity is below 90 percent, this is a restricted margin account. The retention requirement placed a heavy burden on an investor who desired to sell securities and use the proceeds for something other than the purchase of securities. For example, if a customer wanted to withdraw $10,000 from his account, he would have to sell $20,000 worth of securities. Keep in mind, the customer deposited 90 percent for purchase and received only 50 percent on the sale. It wasn't long before a loophole was discovered. The customer would sell $10,000 worth of securities and purchase $10,000 worth of U.S. government securities (also called *exempt securities* because they are exempt from the various rules and regulations, including this 50 percent retention requirement). Consequently, the subsequent sale of the Treasury securities would release the entire $10,000, and the cost to the customer would be just the additional commission on the purchase and sale of the Treasury securities—commissions on Treasury securities are very small.

Needless to say, when the Federal Reserve discovered this practice, they took steps to close this loophole. They established two new accounts: the special convertible debt securities account and the special bond account. By establishing a separate bond account for Treasury and municipals as well as listed corporate debt securities, the loophole would be closed. The reason for establishing an entirely separate account for the listed convertible bond was that this security is a hybrid—part bond, part equity—because of its ability to change from a debt instrument into an equity instrument.

The special convertible debt security account and the special bond account were eliminated on November 23, 1983, and these securities once again became eligible for trading in the customer's margin account. Having these extra accounts was cumbersome and confusing. In addition, these accounts were not permitted to have SMAs attached to them, again requiring journal entries to preserve buying power.

Listed convertible debt securities now have the same margin requirements as listed equity securities—50 percent on initial purchases, 50 percent release on sales, and the same entries to the customer's SMA. In fact, the New York Stock Exchange has the same minimum maintenance requirement for both: 25 percent of the current market value.

The remaining debt instruments we will discuss are listed nonconvertible corporate bonds and exempt securities. Exempt securities include direct obligations of the U.S. government such as Treasury bills, Treasury notes, and Treasury bonds, or any agency guaranteed as to interest or principal by the U.S. government. In addition, municipal bonds (munis) issued by political subdivisions of the United States such as New York state, New Jersey, California, or any other state or city obligation are exempt.

U.S. GOVERNMENT SECURITIES

As stated earlier, direct obligations of the U.S. government are exempt and are not subject to Regulation T. However, the NYSE has initial and minimum maintenance requirements that went into effect on September 1, 1987. These requirements are a sliding scale requiring less as the instrument approaches maturity. The following table gives the requirement for Treasury bills and interest-bearing notes and bonds.

Years to Maturity	NYSE Requirement (% of Market Value)
Less than 1 year	1%
1 year but less than 3 years	2%
3 years but less than 5 years	3%
5 years but less than 10 years	4%
10 years but less than 20 years	5%
20 years or more	6%

ZERO-COUPON GOVERNMENT OBLIGATIONS

Bonds usually have a face amount or principal of $1,000 at maturity as well as a fixed amount of interest usually payable semi-annually. This interest is either paid directly by the issuer to the owner of the bond, if it is a registered bond, or the owner clips interest coupons attached to the bonds and presents them to a paying agent to collect the interest. The latter may be a registered bond but is usually a bearer bond.

A zero-coupon government obligation is a government note or bond where all the coupons have been removed. Therefore, no interest will be paid during the life of the security. At maturity, it will be redeemed at the face value. Since no interest will be paid, this instrument trades at a deep discount from its face value depending on the number of years to maturity. In many respects it is like a savings bond; you pay $25 for it but get back $50 at maturity.

All bonds whether corporate, government, or municipal trade at a percentage of par which is $1,000. A price of 100 means 100 percent of par value or $1,000. A quote on a Treasury note may be "bid, 98.4, ask 98.8". That is a percentage of $1,000 on the bid that would be 98.4/32 percent of $1,000, or $981.25. Government notes and bonds trade in 32nds as opposed to corporates which trade in 1/8ths.

Initial and Maintenance Requirements on Zero-Coupon Government Obligations

Years to Maturity	Requirements
5 or more	3% of principal
more than 5 but less than 10	3% of principal or 4% of market (whichever is greater)
more than 10 but less than 20	3% of principal or 5% of market (whichever is greater)
more than 20	3% of principal or 6% of market (whichever is greater)

Bonds

Example: A customer purchases $10,000 of zero-coupon U.S. Treasury bonds maturing 2/15/05, selling at 32 (total cost: $3,200) in a margin account with existing positions as indicated below. The requirement would be 3 percent of principal ($300) or 5 percent of the market value ($160), whichever is greater ($300). After the purchase the account would appear:

100	B	35	$3,500
200	C	40	8,000
100	D	50	5,000
100	E	35	3,500
10,000 U.S. Treasury bonds 2/15/05 @32			3,200

Market value	$23,200
Debit balance	15,200
Equity	8,000

SMA

Date	Debit	Credit	Balance	Explanation
1/15/88		$2,000	$2,000	sale 100 A@40

Notice that there is no entry (debit) to the customer's SMA, and no Regulation T call was issued, because there is no Federal Reserve requirement. The $300 requirement is a NYSE initial and maintenance requirement and is already in the account.

Req.	Eq.
$5,000	$8,300
300	−5,300
$5,300	$2,700 excess over NYSE req.

The $5,000 requirement is 25 percent of the current market value of the equity securities that were already in the margin account. The $300 requirement is 3 percent of the principal amount on the newly purchased zero-coupon government obligation. While no deposit was required on the purchase of the zero-coupon government obligation, nothing will be released to the SMA when it is sold, either. However, you may always recompute the account and give the customer any excess.

The same principal applies when purchasing other direct government obligations—there are no Federal Reserve requirements and the NYSE requirements are the same as those stated earlier.

Most investors would not purchase a large amount of government securities using the minimum requirements, because the interest charged on the debit balance would exceed the yield on the security. However, a customer might have $100,000 fully paid for 9 ¼ percent Treasury notes due May 1990 trading at par and need to borrow $95,000 for a business venture for six months. The customer may very well use these securities as collateral.

MUNICIPALS

Generally, municipal securities fall into one of two categories. The first, *general obligations,* are backed by the full faith and credit of the issuer. The second, *revenue bonds,* are not backed by the municipalities, but rather by the revenue generated by a particular facility, e.g., the Triborough Bridge and Tunnel Authority bonds, or the Meadowlands Sports Complex. Neither of these bonds are guaranteed by their respective states of New York and New Jersey. The money needed to meet the interest and principal payments to the bondholders must come from the revenue generated by operating each facility. Should the revenue not be sufficient to pay the interest and principal, the bonds would go into default. Therefore, only general obligations may be purchased on margin and carried on a credit basis in a margin account.

Remember, municipal securities are also classified as exempt, and no requirement is imposed by the Federal Reserve or Regulation T. However, the NYSE has initial and maintenance requirements, which are 15 percent of the market value or 7 percent of the principal (whichever amount is greater). When do these initial requirements take effect? If a customer purchased 10 M ($10,000) NYC 8 ½ of 95 @87, a requirement is established for 15 percent of the market value ($1,305) or 7 percent of the principal ($700), whichever is greater (in this case $1,305).

Bonds

The requirement for municipals will usually be 15 percent of the market value. This is because in order for the 7 percent requirement to be the larger of the two, the market value of the bond would have to be 46 ⅝ or lower, which would mean the interest rate would be around 2 percent, and the bond would have had to be issued a long time ago. Very few such bonds are around. However, should interest rates rise sharply, bond prices will fall, and the 7 percent of principal could become a factor.

Let's look at our margin account and see what happens with a purchase of 10 NYC 8 ½ of 95 @87.

100	B			35	$3,500
200	C			40	8,000
100	D			50	5,000
100	E			35	3,500
10	M	U.S. Treasury bonds 2/15/05		@32	3,200
10	M	NYC 8 ½ 95		@87	8,700

	Market value	$31,900
	Debit balance	23,900
	Equity	8,000

SMA

Date	Debit	Credit	Balance	Explanation
1/15/88		$2,000	$2,000	sale 100 A@40

Again, no change occurs in the SMA because there is no Regulation T requirement. However, looking at the size of the customer's debit balance, is it possible that the account may require funds for the New York Stock Exchange?

Req.	Eq.
$5,000	$8,000
300	−6,605
1,305	1,395 excess over NYSE Req.
$6,605	

Our account is fine, since there is an excess of $1,395. The requirements were arrived at by taking 25 percent of the market value of the four stocks (25% × $20,000 = $5000), plus 3 percent of the zero-coupon government obligation (3% × $10,000 = $300), plus 15 percent of the market value of the municipal security, (15% × $8700 = $1305).

Carrying this a step further, let's assume the market value of the securities increases as follows:

100	B		55	$5,500
200	C		43	8,600
100	D		60	6,000
100	E		41	4,100
10	M	U.S. Treasury bonds 2/15/05	@42	4,200
10	M	NYC 8 ½ 95	@92	9,200

Market value	$37,600
Debit balance	23,900
Equity	13,700

SMA

Date	Debit	Credit	Balance	Explanation
1/15/88		$2,000	$2,000	sale 100 A@40

And recomputing for Regulation T:

Req.	Eq.
$12,000	$13,700
	−12,100
	$1,800 excess over Reg. T

Notice that under the Req. column we are only using a figure of $12,100. This represents 50 percent of the market value of the stock in the account. The $10,000 of U.S. Treasury bonds and the $10,000 of NYC bonds are exempt securities having no Regulation T requirement.

Bonds

NONCONVERTIBLE CORPORATE BONDS

Nonconvertible bonds sometimes are referred to as straight corporate debt securities. Nonconvertible bonds are eligible for purchase in the margin account if they are listed on a national securities exchange or included on the list published by the Federal Reserve. Margin requirements for these securities are a bit odd. Regulation T allows brokers (creditors) to establish their own margin requirements for straight corporate bonds and accepts whatever that requirement is as the Fed's. Therefore, one broker may charge 40 percent of the market value and another broker 25 percent of the market value. On the other hand, the NYSE also has initial and maintenance requirements for nonconvertible bonds: 20 percent of the market value or 7 percent of the principal, whichever amount is greater. These, then, become the minimum requirements. Effectively, a broker could require more than the NYSE minimum, but no less.

For any listed bond selling above 35, the requirement will be 20 percent of the market value. The requirement for any bond selling below 35 will be 7 percent of the principal or face amount. At 35, the requirements are the same—$70 based on a $1,000 bond.

Back to our customer, currently as follows:

100	B		55	$5,500
200	C		43	8,600
100	D		60	6,000
100	E		41	4,100
10	M	U.S. Treasury bonds 2/15/05	@42	4,200
10	M	NYC 8 ½ 95	@92	9,200

Market value	$37,600
Debit balance	23,900
Equity	13,700

SMA

Date	Debit	Credit	Balance	Explanation
1/15/88		$2,000	$2,000	sale 100 A@40

If this customer now purchases 10 Ford Motor credit bonds 8 ½ due 2001 @ 87 ½, the account will look like this:

100	B			55	$5,500
200	C			43	8,600
100	D			60	6,000
100	E			41	4,100
10	M	U.S. Treasury bonds 2/15/05		@42	4,200
10	M	NYC 8 ½ 95		@92	9,200
10	M	Ford Motor credit 8 ⅜ 01		@87½	8,750

Market value	$46,350
Debit balance	32,650
Equity	13,700

Now this purchase has a Regulation T requirement of the greater of 20 percent of the market value: $1,750; or 7 percent of the principal ($700). $1,750 is the NYSE requirement, but because of the language in Regulation T, it becomes a Federal call. Since funds are available in the SMA, the entry is as follows:

SMA

Date	Debit	Credit	Balance	Explanation
1/15/88		$2,000	$2,000	sale 100 A@40
1/27/88	$1,750		250	pur. 10 MFord

Look at our account. Again, that debit looks large, and the account should be refigured for NYSE.

Req.	Eq.
$6,050	$13,700
300	− 9,480
1,380	$4,220 excess over NYSE min.
1,750	maintenance requirement
$9,480	

All we are doing is taking each item separately. The $6,050 represents 25 percent of the current market value of the equity securities (the stocks) in the margin account; $300 is the requirement of 3 percent of the principal amount of the zero-coupon government obligation; $1,380 is the requirement of 15 percent of the market value of the municipal bond; and $1,750 is the requirement of 20 percent of the market value of the listed corporate debt security. Remember that 20 percent of the market value of the corporate bond is both a Federal initial requirement and an NYSE minimum maintenance requirement.

Effective September 15, 1988, the Federal Reserve Board announced that Regulation T had been amended to allow U.S. brokers to extend credit on certain foreign sovereign debt securities. The effect of this amendment is to allow loan value on long-term debt securities issued or guaranteed as a general obligation by a foreign sovereign. In order for these securities to be eligible, the foreign sovereign debt instruments must be rated by Standard & Poor's or Moody's and given one of the two highest ratings, AA or AAA. The securities in question may be treated the same as OTC margin bonds.

According to Regulation T, good faith loan value is sufficient. However, members of the NYSE or NASD would be subject to the greater of 20 percent of the current market value or 7 percent of the principal of the bond in question.

The following is a copy of the amendment.

2. Section 220.0 is amended by adding a new paragraph (r) (4) to read:

220.2 Definitions

* * * * * *

(r) "OTC margin bond" means: * *

(4) A debt security issued or guaranteed as a general obligation by the government of a foreign country, its provinces, states, or cities, or a supernational entity, if at the time of the extension of credit one of the following is rated in one of the two highest rating categories by a nationally recognized statistical rating organization:

(i) the issue,

(ii) the issuer or guarantor (implicitly), or

(iii) other outstanding unsecured long-term debt securities issued or guaranteed by the government or entity.

CHAPTER SIX QUESTIONS

1. The NYSE minimum maintenance requirements for the long position in listed convertible bonds is:
   a. $2,000.
   b. 50 percent of the market value.
   c. no NYSE requirements.
   d. 25 percent or the market value.

2. A purchase of a Treasury bill has a Regulation T requirement of:
   a. 5 percent of the principal amount.
   b. 1 percent of the market value.
   c. 15 percent of the market value.
   d. no Regulation T requirement.

3. The purchase of a NYC G.O. bond has a NYSE requirement of:
   a. 15 percent of the market value or 7 percent of the principal whichever is greater.
   b. 25 percent of the market value.
   c. 5 percent of the principal amount.
   d. No requirement; it is classified as an exempt security.

4. If a customer deposits a fully paid for Treasury note maturing in two years the broker may lend the customer:
   a. 50 percent of the market value.
   b. 98 percent of the market value.
   c. 3 percent of the market value.
   d. 25 percent of the market value.

Bonds

5. Exempt securities are:
   a. direct obligations of the United States.
   b. municipal bonds.
   c. an agency guaranteed as to principal or interest by the United States.
   d. all of the above.

6. A purchase of a municipal revenue bond requires a deposit of:
   a. 100 percent of the market value.
   b. 15 percent of the market value or 7 percent of the principal whichever amount is greater.
   c. 50 percent of the market value.
   d. 25 percent of the market value.

7. The settlement date on purchases of U.S. government obligations is:
   a. five business days.
   b. seven business days.
   c. the next business day.
   d. two business days after the trade date known as a skip settlement.

8. A purchase of a zero-coupon government bond maturing in 22 years requires a NYSE maintenance requirement of:
   a. no requirement.
   b. 3 percent of the principal or 6 percent of the market value whichever is greater.
   c. 3 percent of the principal.
   d. 50 percent of the market value.

9. A customer purchases $100,000 of Canadian debt securities, the required Regulation T margin is:
   a. 20 percent of the market value or 7 percent of the principal amount, whichever is greater.
   b. full payment is required.
   c. 50 percent—same as listed securities.
   d. no margin, treat the same as U.S. government obligations.

10. Foreign sovereign debt must be rated by a recognized investment service in which rating?
   a. AA or A.
   b. The top tour rating, making them bank quality.
   c. AA or AAA.
   d. A or above.

Chapter Seven

MISCELLANEOUS CATEGORIES

This chapter discusses areas that the Margin Department is responsible for but are either dealt with infrequently or have been automated.

WHEN-ISSUED AND WHEN-DISTRIBUTED TRANSACTIONS

A *when-issued* transaction is a trade in a security that has not yet been issued and in reality is a *when-as-and-if-issued* transaction. There is no guarantee that a security trading on a when-issued basis will in fact be issued. A security will be traded on a when-issued basis in several situations. If a company announces plans to split the stock, the old security will trade at one price and the new security (if it were a two-for-one split) would trade at one-half the price of the old security. While the plan for the split has been announced, it still must be approved by the stockholders, the SEC, etc. When one company announces plans to merge with another, the new security often starts trading on a when-issued basis. There have been times when the deal was all set to be completed and the U.S Justice Department stepped in at the last moment and declared the merger in violation of antitrust laws. When this happens, the when-issued contract is canceled and the deal is canceled. Any profits that a customer may have are eliminated, as well as any losses. On the other hand, once the deal has been approved by all parties, the securities start trading on a *regular-way* basis. When-issued securities are "unissued" and are referred to as such under Regulation T.

An interesting specific example of when-issued trading was the break-up of the American Telephone and Telegraph Company. Under government orders to divest themselves of local operating companies, the following companies were spun off:

NYNEX
Pacific Telesis
Southwestern Bell
U.S. West
Ameritech
BellSouth
Bell Atlantic

Because of the size of this company and the millions of shares involved, these seven new companies traded on a when-issued basis for a number of months, until the new securities became available.

In a customer's cash account, purchases of when-issued securities may be made, but full payment is not required until seven business days after the security is available for delivery (begin trading regular way). However, there are deposit requirements under NYSE Rule 431. The purchase of a when-issued contract in a customer's cash account requires a deposit of 25 percent or $2,000, whichever is greater. In the event full payment is less than $2,000, full payment must be received promptly (five business days). Consequently, a customer who purchases $10,000 of when-issued securities in his cash account would require no funds as far as Regulation T is concerned but would be required to deposit $2,500 to satisfy the NYSE requirement. This is the same as the initial requirement of $2,000 and minimum maintenance requirement of 25 percent for a margin account. In fact, a customer may be able to

Miscellaneous Categories

purchase a when-issued security without depositing any additional funds. Suppose a customer had existing accounts as follows:

Customer's Cash Account

Market Value (long) Securities $20,000

Customer's Margin Account

Market value	$10,000
Debit balance	5,000
Equity	5,000

If this customer purchased $10,000 of when-issued securities in his cash account, no deposit would be required since the required funds are already in the account.

	Req.	*Eq.*
25% of M.V. in cash acct.	$5,000	$20,000
25% req. on when-issued	2,500	0
25% req. on margin acct.	2,500	+5,000
	$10,000	25,000
		−10,000
		$15,000 excess over NYSE req.

In our example, the customer has an excess of $15,000 over the NYSE requirement.

A word of caution: while in the above example the deposit of $2,500 would not have to be made, full cash payment is still required seven business days after the security starts trading on a regular-way basis. In the event the customer sells the when-issued securities prior to depositing the full cash payment, the cash account becomes frozen for 90 calendar days.

Now let's assume that after our customer purchases a when-issued security for $10,000, the price increases to $11,000, and he wishes to sell it while it is still trading on a when-issued basis. To avoid the 90-day freeze, the customer must now deposit the entire $10,000, representing the full cash payment. After the sale, the only funds that could be returned to the customer would be the deposit of $10,000. The $1,000, representing the profit, would be retained until the fifth business day after the security started trading on a regular-way basis, which would be the settlement date for the when-issued contract.

The reason for the retention of the profit is the possibility of the contract being canceled. If it was canceled, the $1,000 profit would be eliminated. Keep in mind that when-issued contracts do not settle until they are actually issued. Suppose the price drops to $9,000, and the customer wishes to sell it while it is still trading on a when-issued basis. To avoid the 90-day freeze, the customer would have to deposit the full cost ($10,000). If the sale was made for $9,000, the release to the customer would be $9,000. The $1,000 loss would be held by the broker until settlement date. In the event the when-issued security was canceled, the $1,000 would be returned to the customer and no loss would be sustained.

Purchases of when-issued securities in a customer's margin account are treated the same as any other issued, listed security. Section 220.5(a)(1) of Regulation T states: "The required margin on a net long or short commitment in an unissued security is the margin that would be required if the security were an issued margin security." Therefore, purchases in the customer's margin account require a deposit of 50 percent of the market value. This is the one instance that cash account requirements are lower than margin account requirements. The procedure of retaining any profits or losses until the security goes the regular way is exactly the same for margin accounts as for cash accounts.

MARKS TO THE MARKET

When-issued securities are also subject to marks to the market. This is particularly true when the when-issued contract will be open for a long period of time. The recent break-up of American Telephone and Telegraph into new companies resulted in the new companies trading on a when-issued basis for nine months. A mark to the market occurs when the price changes. In our first example, the customer purchased $10,000 of a when-issued security, and the price increased to $11,000. The broker would charge or debit the selling broker $1,000 to protect his customer. In the event the selling broker went out of business, we would have sufficient funds to repurchase the security and make the customer whole. A mark to the market against us would occur if, after we purchased a when-issued contract, the market value declined.

WHEN-DISTRIBUTED SECURITIES

When-distributed securities are far less common than when-issued securities. The only difference is that a when-distributed security is in fact an issued security, just not distributed as yet. This transaction occurs when a company that owns another company decides to distribute the securities to its shareholders. The physical requirement of printing certificates and breaking them down into the proper denominations takes time. Consequently, the security will trade on a when-distributed basis. They are treated the same as a when-issued security as far as purchases and sales in the customers' cash and margin accounts.

SEGREGATION OF CUSTOMERS' SECURITIES

One of the most important rules, not only from the brokers' and regulatory agencies' standpoint, but also from the customers', is the requirement that the broker segregate customers' securities.

As you may know, one of the services that a broker performs is keeping custody of customers' securities. The advantages of such a service are numerous. The securities are in a safe place; the securities are more likely to be delivered promptly when sales are made, dividends and other distributions are easier to distribute, and the customers' securities are insured by the federally chartered organization known as Securities Investors' Protection Corporation. Most brokers don't charge a custody fee for this service. However, the broker is in a good position. If the security is sold, it will probably be sold by the broker holding the security, thereby assuring him a commission on the sale. While there are definite advantages to holding the customers' securities, certain restrictions must be strictly adhered to.

Fully paid-for customers' securities must be completely segregated. *Segregated* is the term used on Wall Street for safekeeping or locking up customers' securities. Therefore, if a customer purchases securities in his cash account, when the securities are received and paid for, they must be identified as to whom they belong and then placed into segregation. Fully paid-for securities must be placed into segregation even if they are to remain in *street name* (held in the broker's name as opposed to the actual individual's name). In this regard, each broker must maintain a *stock record*—a record that shows the position and location of all the securities that the broker is responsible for. This record is truly the heart and lungs of the brokerage operation.

REVIEW OF CUSTOMER'S ACCOUNTS

Brokerage firms are subject to examination by each of the following organizations:

New York Stock Exchange (if members).
National Association of Security Dealers.
The Securities and Exchange Commission.
An audit once a year by an outside certified public accountant
Internal audits.

Each examining staff will first check the brokerage firm's net capital and then its stock record to see if customers' fully paid-for securities are in fact segregated as required. Failure to comply with this requirement can lead to substantial fines and suspensions.

What about securities that are not fully paid for? A portion of the securities held in a margin account may be used to finance the debit as follows:

Customer's Margin Account

Market value	$35,000
Debit balance	15,000
Equity	20,000

Miscellaneous Categories

In most instances, a broker carrying the above account would finance the customer's debit balance by going to a bank and borrowing the $15,000. Brokers borrow from banks at what is known as the *Broker's Call Rate*—a secured demand loan, hence the name. This loan is secured by pledging a portion of the customer's securities.

The actual segregation rule requires the broker to segregate anything in excess of 140 percent of the debit balance. In other words, the broker must segregate or lock up $14,000 of the customer's securities. The remaining $21,000 (140% × $15,000 = $21,000) may be placed as collateral with the bank. The reason for this rather odd percentage is that banks will lend from 70 percent to 75 percent of the value of the security depending on its quality. Therefore, in our example, the brokerage firm's stock record would show $21,000 in bank loan and $14,000 in segregation. This rule is aimed at protecting the customer. Let's look at our account again:

Customer's Margin Account

Market value	$35,000
Debit balance	15,000
Equity	20,000

Location of customer's securities:

| *Bank Loan* | *Segregation Vault* |
| $21,000 | $14,000 |

In the event that the brokerage house went bankrupt, the bank holding the securities securing the loan of $15,000 would liquidate the securities to obtain payment of their $15,000 loan. The remaining $6,000 would be turned over to the liquidator (Securities Investor Protection Corporation), SIPC. The remaining $14,000 of securities that were properly placed in segregation would give the customer a combined total of $20,000, which is exactly the customer's equity or ownership in the account.

In this regard, when a customer opens a margin account, he must sign a margin agreement, which describes in detail the various requirements and responsibilities. Upon reading the agreement, there is a provision for the rehypothecation of customer securities. *Rehypothecation* means to repledge. In the above example, the repledging of $21,000 of the customer's securities to the bank to secure the loan of $15,000 is also known as rehypothecation of the customer's securities.

Earlier we mentioned stock loans. Remember, when a broker lends securities for stock loans, the broker usually gets 100 percent of the market value as collateral. Using our example:

Customer's Margin Account

Market value	$35,000
Debit balance	15,000
Equity	20,000

If our broker lends the customer's securities for a stock loan and receives 100 percent of the market value, the stock record for the customer's securities would show the following:

Stock Loan	*Segregation or Vault*
$15,000	$20,000

Since our broker received $15,000 in cash to collateralize the loan of $15,000 of securities, our broker would now be required to segregate the remaining $20,000 of securities.

INTEREST CHARGES

As you can imagine, a margin account is a credit account where a customer pays for a portion of the securities and the broker, referred to as a "creditor" under Regulation T, finances the remainder. As we have stated, the current requirement under Regulation T is 50 percent. This means that a purchase of $10,000 of securities requires a deposit of $5,000. The broker is financing the remaining $5,000—a loan to the customer.

As a general rule brokers must borrow the money from a bank to finance this purchase. As previously stated in this chapter, brokers borrow money from banks at the *broker's call rate* and then add a

Miscellaneous Categories

minimum one half of one percent when charging a customer interest on the loan made to him. For debit balances under $50,000, generally the interest rate charged will be more.

The customer must be advised of how much the charges will be when due and how they must be paid. This is usually done in the customer's margin account agreement. There are several rules, laws and regulations that require this information to be disclosed: Securities and Exchange Commission Rule 10 (b) 16, Regulation Z of the Federal Reserve System, and the so-called Truth in Lending Law of 1968.

The above rules, regulations, and laws are lengthy, wordy, and complicated, but we will try to simplify them.

Interest rates are based on an annual rate and interest due is calculated by using the following formula:

$$\text{Interest} = \text{Principal} \times \text{Rate} \times \text{Time}$$

The amount of interest charged is reflected in the customer's monthly statement. This statement reflects all the customer's transactions for the previous month along with the current holdings—both long and short. In a statement for a margin account, there is a debit charge titled "interest" or "interest charges," which will increase the debit balance by that amount. The date that interest is charged will vary from firm to firm. Usually the interest is charged on the 15th of the month and the statement cut-off date may be some time after that—e.g., the 20th of each month. Let's assume our customer's margin account has the following balances:

Market value	$100,000
Debit balance	60,000
Equity	40,000

First, note that in our example the account is restricted. The debit balance is in excess of $50,000; therefore, the broker is only charging the minimum interest of one half of one percent above the broker's call rate. If broker's call rate is currently 8 ½, percent, when we add one half of one percent, the actual charge to the customer will be 9 percent. Therefore, on the 15th of the month the broker would increase the customer's debit by $450 ($60,000 × 9% × $\frac{30}{360}$ days). The broker's actual cost of funds was $425 ($60,000 × 8.5% × $\frac{30}{360}$ days). The broker's mark-up is minimal: $25 per month. However, where the broker can really make money is through the stock loan program. By using available securities in house and getting 100 percent of the market value in cash for a stock loan, he is now able to finance his own customer's debit balance.

Instead of borrowing from the bank, he may use stock loans and get the money "free" and charge the margin customer the same 9 percent. Since he has no cost of funds, the $450 charged in the above example is pure profit for the broker.

The customer's account after the charge will look like this:

Market value	$100,000
Debit balance	60,450
Equity	39,550

The charge of $450 would not create a Federal Call requiring the customer to deposit additional funds, even though the increase in the debit further restricts the margin account.

MARGIN ON NEW ISSUES

The Securities and Exchange Commission has ruled that credit cannot be extended on new issues until 30 days after the syndicate was closed. This means that brokers are not allowed to finance or let their customers buy new issues on margin—for good reason. Underwriters are anxious to sell the securities they are issuing in order to close out the syndicate and get on to another deal. Should a particular underwriting be going poorly, an underwriter may be tempted to convince his customer to take more securities than he should by placing them in his margin account. The SEC's ruling prevents this occurrence.

This created a problem on certain investment company securities. Closed-end investment companies presented no problem if they

Miscellaneous Categories

were listed or on the Federal Reserve's over-the-counter marginable list and were over 30 days old after the syndicate was closed; they would be eligible for margin. However, open-end investment companies (mutual funds) presented a different problem. Purchases of these securities are direct from the fund itself. Consequently, the SEC ruled that these purchases are a continuing *new issue*. However, if a customer has held the securities for 30 days, they may be transferred from the customer's cash account (where they would have been required to be purchased) to the customer's margin account, where the broker may extend 50 percent loan value on the securities.

However, there is one exception to this: if the customer purchased open-end investment share (mutual funds) elsewhere (through another broker), they are immediately eligible for the margin account and may have credit extended on them.

DAY TRADES

A *day trade* is the purchase and sale of the same security on the same day. Under Regulation T, no deposit is required if there is no increase in the customer's debit balance at the end of the day. Assume the customer's account is as follows:

Market value	$30,000
Debit balance	17,000
Equity	13,000

If this customer purchased $10,000 of securities in this account and sold the same $10,000 of securities later in the day with neither a profit nor a loss, there would be no Regulation T requirement.

Account after the purchase of $10,000

Market value	$40,000
Debit balance	27,000
Equity	13,000

Account after the sale of $10,000

Market value	$30,000
Debit balance	17,000
Equity	13,000

As you can see, no change occurs in the customer's debit balance from the beginning of the day to the end. Consequently, there is no Regulation T requirement.

The chance that a customer would buy and sell a security on one day with no change in price is remote. However, if a loss of $500 or less were incurred this would constitute a Regulation T call. But the amount may be waived at the broker's discretion. Profits may be placed in the customer's SMA.

The major regulatory agency governing day trades is the New York Stock Exchange, which has two different requirements, one for so-called day traders and the other for non-day traders. A day trader is any customer whose trading shows a pattern of day trading. The Exchange considers a pattern to mean day trades took place on *more* than three different days in a 12-month period. A non-day trader is defined as customer who has day traded *no more* than three different days in a 12-month period. Therefore, if a customer day traded four or more days in a 12-month period, he is a day trader; three or less and he is a non-day trader.

Both day traders and non-day traders are required to have a minimum equity in their respective margin accounts of at least $2,000.

Requirements for a Day Trader

Let's use our earlier example:

Market value	$30,000
Debit balance	17,000
Equity	13,000

The New York Stock Exchange requires maintenance excess equal to the initial Regulation T requirement for the highest position held at any time during the day.

Miscellaneous Categories

Req.	Eq.
$7,500	$13,000
	− 7,500
	$5,500 excess over maintenance requirement.

If this customer purchased $10,000 in listed securities and sold the same $10,000 of securities on the same day, he would not be required to deposit any additional funds. This is because the initial requirement under Regulation T is currently 50 percent for purchased securities, and, therefore, the maintenance requirement under NYSE rules is $5,000. The excess over the minimum requirement was $5,500.

What if our customer purchases and sells $15,000 in securities on the same day?

```
50% of $15,000         = $7,500
Excess over NYSE
  minimum req.            5,500
NYSE day trade call     $2,500
```

This customer must deposit $2,500 within seven business days to meet the call. An important note: the $2,500 is a New York Stock Exchange call, not a Regulation T call. No funds are required as far as Regulation T is concerned. Therefore, when the funds are deposited, the debit balance is reduced and the $2,500 is credited to the customer's SMA. As far as the SMA is concerned, these funds can be withdrawn in the future.

Let's look at the customer's account after the deposit:

```
Market value        $30,000
Debit balance        14,500
Equity               15,500
```

SMA

Date	Debit	Credit	Balance	Explanation
1/18/88		$2,500	$2,500	Deposit of funds

The requirements for a non-day trader are simply that at least 25 percent minimum maintenance be kept in the account. An example:

Market value	$30,000
Debit balance	17,000
Equity	13,000

How much can this customer day trade without requiring additional margin? The formula is 4 × the equity minus the current market value.

$$4 \times \$13,000 = \$52,000$$
$$-30,000 \text{ current market value}$$
$$\$22,000$$

This customer could purchase and sell $22,000 of securities without depositing additional funds. To explain, let's look at the customer's margin account after the purchase:

Market value	$52,000
Debit balance	39,000
Equity	13,000

Recompute the account:

Req.	Eq.
$13,000	$13,000

As you can see, this account is exactly at the 25 percent New York Stock Exchange minimum maintenance level.

Using the same example again:

Market value	$30,000
Debit balance	17,000
Equity	13,000

A non-day trader buys for $15,000 and sells for $14,000. The account would look like this after the purchase:

Market value	$45,000
Debit balance	32,000
Equity	13,000

After the sale the account would appear thus:

Market value	$30,000
Debit balance	18,000
Equity	12,000

Note that as a result of the loss, the debit balance was increased by $1,000, which would represent a Federal or Regulation T call.

CHAPTER SEVEN QUESTIONS

The following questions concern cash and margin accounts. The questions are to be considered a final exam, to test your understanding. Good Luck.

1. A customer sells short 100 ABC @18 as the first transaction in a margin account. The initial requiremnt for Regulation T is 50 percent. A call should be sent to the customer for what amount?
    a. $900.
    b. $2,000.
    c. $1,800.
    d. $2,500.

2. A customer's account is as follows:

Market value	$17,000
Debit balance	9,000
Equity	8,000

SMA balance of $3,000

The customer makes a purchase of $9,000 of listed securities. How much cash must the customer deposit?
a. $4,500.
b. $6,000.
c. $1,500.
d. $3,000.

3. Using the account and transaction in question 2, if the customer wished to bring in listed securities to meet the Regulation T call, how much must he deposit?
a. $3,000.
b. $4,500.
c. $18,000.
d. $9,000.

4. A customer sells short 100 XYZ @50 and deposits the required margin. Sometime thereafter, the price of XYZ rises to 55. Show the account after the appropriate mark to the market.
a. Market value $5,500.
b. Market value $5,000.
c. Credit balance $3,500.
d. Credit balance   0.

5. A customer purchases a security in his cash account, which is subsequently liquidated for nonpayment, and the account is frozen for the next 90 days. What is the effect of this freeze?
a. No further transactions are allowed in this account for the next 90 days.
b. Only sales are permitted. Purchases are not permitted under any circumstances.
c. The customer's name is placed on file with the NYSE and he is not permitted to trade for 90 calendar days.
d. The customer must have sufficient funds to pay for the purchase prior to the trade being executed for the next 90 calendar days.

Questions 6, 7, and 8 pertain to the following margin account:

Market value	$63,500
Debit balance	41,200

Miscellaneous Categories

6. What is the equity in this customer's account?
   a. $22,300.
   b. $31,750.
   c. $15,875.
   d. None of the above.

7. What is the excess maintenance in the customer's account?
   a. $15,875.
   b. $6,425.
   c. $31,750.
   d. $9,450.

8. What is the maintenance requirement in the customer's account?
   a. $15,875.
   b. $6,000.
   c. $9,450.
   d. $31,750.

9. Assume the initial Regulation T requirement is 70 percent and this is customer's account:

   | Market value | $60,000 |
   | Debit balance | 12,000 |

   What is the Regulation T excess?
   a. $12,000.
   b. $18,000.
   c. $48,000.
   d. $6,000.

10. Using the same account and initial requirement as in question 9, what would be the customer's buying power?
    a. $12,000.
    b. $8,571.
    c. The customer has no buying power.
    d. $3,000.

11. Initial margin requirements are established by which regulatory organization?
    a. The SEC.
    b. The SIPC.
    c. The Federal Reserve.
    d. The MSRB.

Questions 12 and 13 pertain to the following margin account:
　　　　Market value　　　　$10,000
　　　　Debit balance　　　　 8,000
　　　　SMA balance　　　　 5,000

12. What is the maintenance call?
    a. 0.
    b. $2,000.
    c. $3,000.
    d. $500.

13. How much in securities would have to be sold to bring the account into compliance with the NYSE minimum maintenance requirements?
    a. $500.
    b. $1,000.
    c. $2,000.
    d. $3,000.

14. Which law requires a plus tick or zero-plus tick for short sales of listed securities?
    a. The Securities Act of 1933.
    b. The Securities Exchange Act of 1934.
    c. The Maloney Act.
    d. The Securities Investors Protection Act.

15. In order for a security to be purchased in a margin account, the security must be:
    I. listed on a national securities exchange.
    II. traded over-the-counter.
    III. on the list published by the Federal Reserve.
    IV. listed on the Toronto Stock Exchange.

a. I.
b. I and II.
c. III and IV.
d. I and III.

16. A customer sells $10,000 of listed securities in a restricted margin account. How much may be released?
    a. $5,000.
    b. $2,000.
    c. $10,000.
    d. $3,000.

17. A business day is defined as:
    a. when the banks are open.
    b. any day other than a legal holiday.
    c. when the stock exchanges are open.
    d. Monday, Tuesday, Wednesday, Thursday, and Friday.

18. A customer sells short 1,000 shares of a security selling at $2 a share. This is the initial transaction in the customer's margin account. How much must the customer deposit?
    a. $2,000.
    b. $2,500.
    c. $1,000.
    d. The transaction is not permitted.

19. A customer deposits one fully paid-for general obligation municipal bond selling at 80. How much can the broker lend this customer?
    a. $120.
    b. $400.
    c. $200.
    d. $680.

20. For a short sale against the box, the requirements are:
    a. 10 percent of the long side, keeping the short side marked to the market.
    b. 50 percent of the long side, nothing on the short side
    c. 5 percent of the long side, keeping the short side marked to the market.
    d. none of the above.

21. Which of the following would be classified as "exempt" securities?
    a. U.S. government obligations.
    b. Agencies guaranteed by the U.S. government.
    c. Treasury notes.
    d. All of the above.

22. May a Treasury bill be purchased in the customer's cash account with instructions to send them to the customer?
    a. Yes.
    b. No.

23. Fully paid-for customer's securities being held by the broker:
    a. may be commingled with those securities of the broker.
    b. must be segregated and identified as belonging to the customer.
    c. may be used by the broker for stock loans.
    d. may be hypothecated by the broker.

24. Requests for extensions of time for late payments are requested from which organization?
    a. A Federal Reserve Bank.
    b. The Securities and Exchange Commission.
    c. The New York Stock Exchange.
    d. The Municipal Securities Rule Making Board.

25. A customer purchases $9,000 of listed securities in a restricted margin account. The same day she sells $12,000 in different securities. The permissible withdrawal is:
    a. $6,000.
    b. $1,500.
    c. $4,500.
    d. 0.

Appendix A

THE FEDERAL RESERVE

In discussing purchasing of securities on margin or credit, some background information on the Federal Reserve System is appropriate, since it regulates the amount of credit outstanding in the United States.

Most foreign countries have a central bank that is controlled by their government. The United States has a central bank, but it is not controlled by the government. In fact, parts of the central bank are spread throughout the country, as the United States has usually favored a decentralized type of control.

The Federal Reserve System is divided into 12 different districts throughout the country. If you look at the face of a dollar bill, on the left side you will see a large letter. This letter indicates which Federal Reserve Bank distributed the money, "A" is from Boston, "B" is from New York, and "C" is from Philadelphia. (A complete listing of the Reserve Banks with addresses can be found at the end of this appendix.) The Federal Reserve Banks do not print the money, they simply distribute it.

Remember that the Federal Reserve Bank is not a government agency. It is a bank, but a very special one. It is often called "the banker's bank." Though there is no connection to the federal government, there is governmental influence, as discussed below.

At the top level of the Federal Reserve System, is a board of governors. There are seven governors, and all are appointed by the President of the United States for a 14-year term. The only restriction on appointing a member to the board of governors is that no two governors may come from the same Federal Reserve district. In addition, since the terms are for 14 years, the governors are politically insulated from day-to-day pressures. The president normally appoints a governor every two years. Consequently, many members of the board are appointed by different presidents and political parties, thus many varying economic viewpoints are represented.

The level below the board of governors is the board of directors. Each of the 12 Federal Reserve districts has its own board of directors. Each board of directors consists of nine individuals, three of whom are appointed by the board of governors. However, the remaining six are elected by the member banks in each district. As you can see, two-thirds of each board of directors is controlled by the member banks themselves. Each district also has a slate of officers.

We know that the primary purpose of the Federal Reserve is to regulate the amount of credit outstanding in the United States. Approximately 14,000 commercial banks are in the United States today. About 5,000 of these are members of the Federal Reserve System. How can a mere one-third of the banks be so powerful? These 5,000 member banks are responsible for 75 percent of the available credit in the United States.

How does the Federal Reserve control credit? There are three major and several lesser ways.

RESERVE REQUIREMENTS

As a member of the Federal Reserve System, a bank is required to deposit a percentage of its deposits.

A bank has three basic types of deposits.

1. D.D.A. or demand deposits accounts. This is a fancy name for checking accounts. The bank has no idea when a customer is going to write a check or for what amount. For this reason, the monies in a customer's checking account require

the highest percentage to be left with the Federal Reserve. There is a complex sliding scale formula, but for our use, the percentage is approximately 16 percent.

2. Time deposits (i.e., CDs) require a far smaller deposit, because the bank knows when it must return the borrowed funds and can make the necessary arrangements.

3. Savings deposits require about the same reserve as time deposits, because savings accounts have a tendency to remain for longer periods of time than checking accounts. In addition, the bank has the right to require 30 days' notice prior to any withdrawal. This right is seldom used, but it could become necessary if there were a "run" on the bank. Most people are unaware of this condition, but just read the first page of your passbook. As a member of the Federal Reserve, a bank is required to compute its reserve requirements daily. With the banking industry so highly computerized this task is easily completed.

If at the end of the day, the bank has a $20 million requirement, this is recorded and set aside until Wednesday. Wednesday is the end of the bank week. At this point, the member bank would look at its daily reserve requirement for the previous two weeks and take an average. If it came up with a requirement of $25 million, and there was only $15 million on deposit with the Federal Reserve, it would have to deposit $10 million by the end of the day to be in compliance with the Reserve requirement. Under normal circumstances, it would be very difficult to attract sufficient deposits to satisfy the $10 million requirement. However, other member banks are making the same computation, and some will have excess funds. *Note*: no interest is paid on Federal Reserve deposits, which is one disadvantage in being a member of the Federal Reserve System. Since there is no advantage to leaving excess funds at the Federal Reserve, they become available to be lent to those banks requiring additional deposits. Hence, we get the term *federal funds*, or, more commonly, *Fed funds*.

Members of the Federal Reserve have access to the Federal Reserve wire system, which can move funds from one bank to another in a matter of seconds. So, while the original meaning of Fed funds meant to meet the Reserve's requirements (and still does), Fed funds also has the broader meaning of immediately usable funds, as opposed to clearing house funds.

Clearing-house funds are funds that the average person uses when writing a check to the landlord, the store owner, or a birthday check to someone. The funds are not usable by the recipient until the check clears. The check you wrote goes through the clearing house system, back to the originating bank, which moves the amount out of your account and into the account of the person to whom you wrote the check. If the banks are in the same Federal Reserve district, the check will usually clear the next business day. Checks between districts will take longer, depending on the distance between them.

The *Federal funds rate* is the amount one bank will pay another for the use of funds overnight. This rate is determined by supply and demand. If more banks require funds than have excesses, the Fed fund rate will increase. A classic example of this supply and demand function occurred on December 31, 1986, which also happened to be a Wednesday, the end of the banking week. On this particular day, the Fed fund rate hit a high of 25 percent and a low of ¼ percent. This unusual situation was occasioned by the banks wishing to make some cosmetic changes in the balance sheet for the end of the year. However, the end of the year happened on a Wednesday, and because of these accounting moves, most banks found themselves buyers of Fed funds, which drove the rate to this unusually high rate. By the end of the day, when the banks had settled their requirements with the Federal reserve, there was no demand for these funds, thus the drop to ¼ percent.

With this brief background of Reserve Requirements and Federal Funds, let us look at some of the main ways in which the Federal Reserve regulates credit in the United States.

Reserve Requirements. If the Federal Reserve decided to increase the reserve requirement from 16 percent to 18 percent, this would be a very severe action. All member banks would come under the new additional requirement, and there would be no excess funds to borrow. To attract additional deposits, higher rates would have to

The Federal Reserve

be paid. If additional deposits were not attracted fast enough, *demand* loans would be called, causing liquidations, foreclosures, etc. There is no doubt that increasing the reserve requirements tightens credit. The reverse, lowering reserve requirements, causes the member banks to have excess funds, thereby reducing interest rates and easing credit restraints. Tightening too much causes recessions; easing too much causes inflation. The Federal Reserve strives to strike a balance.

Discount Rate. This is the rate the Federal Reserve charges its member banks to borrow money. The discount rate is historically lower than all other money rates, because the proceeds of the loan are restricted as to use. The member bank may only borrow at the discount rate if the proceeds are used exclusively for meeting the Federal Reserve's requirement. In addition, this loan is a secured loan. The Federal Reserve is willing to help a bank out and lend it money to meet its reserve requirement, but the loan must be collateralized by the very best securities; i.e., Treasury bills, notes, bonds, or those issued by certain government agencies that are guaranteed as to principal or interest. Increasing or decreasing the discount rate has only a very minor effect on the amount of credit available.

Federal Open Market Committee. The actions and decisions of this committee have the most immediate effect on credit availability. Its effect in severity falls somewhere between increasing Reserve requirement and changing the discount rate.

The Federal Open Market Committee comprises the seven governors of the Federal Reserve board and five of the twelve presidents of the various districts throughout the country, one of whom is always the president of the Federal Reserve Bank of New York. The other presidents rotate on and off the committee periodically. This committee meets once a month (more often if needed) and decides the day-to-day credit policy that will be followed. Should the committee decide to tighten credit, this would be accomplished by selling various government obligations to the member banks and charging the banks' respective reserve requirement accounts. This would cause most banks to be below reserve requirements, and monies must be found to replenish their account. Attracting additional deposits requires higher interest rates, which in turn means credit will cost the borrower more.

Now, if the Federal Open Market Committee decides that looser credit policies are in order, the Federal Reserve will start buying the various government bills, notes, and bonds and will pay the banks by crediting their reserve accounts. Then there would be excess reserves in the vast majority of the member banks. With no interest being paid on the funds left with the Federal Reserve, the member banks will withdraw the excess and put it in the hands of the public in the form of loans. To entice the consumer to borrow when there is a surplus of funds, the bank must lower its rate, and the competition must follow. When the FOMC buys, it eases credit and lowers interest rates. The Federal Reserve prefers this method to ease and tighten credit because it is readily reversible.

Other ways the Federal Reserve affects credit are related to the securities industry:

Regulation T.	Regulates the amount of money a broker may lend on securities.
Regulation U.	Regulates the amount of money a bank may lend on securities.
Regulation G.	Regulates the amount of money organizations other than banks and brokers may lend on securities.

There is an additional Regulation, W, which at the direction of the board of governors regulates minimum down payments on household appliances, automobiles, and charge accounts. This Regulation has not been applied since shortly after World War II. However, it is still on the books and was looked at during the years 1979–1980, when the United States was experiencing very high inflation.

Table A–1 Federal Reserve Banks

District	Federal Reserve Bank
1	Boston, Massachusetts 30 Pearl Street (Boston, MA 02106)
2	New York, New York 33 Liberty Street (Federal P.O. Station, New York, NY 14240)
3	Philadelphia, Pennsylvania 925 Chestnut Street (Philadelphia, PA 19101)
4	Cleveland, Ohio 1455 East Sixth Street (P.O. Box 6387, Cleveland, OH 44101)
5	Richmond, Virginia 100 North Ninth Street (P.O. Box 27622, Richmond, VA 23261)
6	Atlanta, Georgia 104 Marietta Street N.W. (Atlanta, GA 30303)
7	Chicago, Illinois 230 LaSalle Street (P.O. Box 834, Chicago, IL 60690)
8	St. Louis, Missouri 411 Locust Street (P.O. Box 442, St. Louis, MO 63166)
9	Minneapolis, Minnesota 73 South Fifth Street (Minneapolis, MN 55480)
10	Kansas City, Missouri 925 Grand Avenue (Federal Reserve Station, Kansas City, MO 64198)
11	Dallas, Texas 400 South Akard Street (Station K, Dallas, TX 75222)
12	San Francisco, California 400 Sansome Street (P.O. Box 7702, San Francisco, CA 94120)

Appendix B

ANSWERS TO CHAPTER QUESTIONS

CHAPTER ONE

1. b   By the seventh business day. While we would prefer the money to be received by the settlement date, the seventh business day is when payment must be received.

2. d   Any time a customer purchases a security and there is a sale of that security without full cash payment being received, that account must be frozen for 90 calendar days.

3. b   Ten business days after settlement is the latest that sold securities must be delivered to the broker.

4. a   The two requirements to use the extended payment for a C.O.D. transaction are (1) instructions of C.O.D. prior to the trade and (2) the reason for the delay, the broker's inability to obtain the securities for delivery.

5. b   The Federal Reserve has given the power to grant extensions of time to the various exchanges and the NASD.

6. c   On the seventh business day after the trade date.

7. c Full cash payment received within the seven business days after the buy automatically lifts the 90-day restriction.

8. d A *regular way* transaction means the trade settles on the fifth business day after the trade date.

9. b The receiving broker must explain why he is DK-ing an item so that the delivering broker can take whatever corrective action may be necessary.

10. b A cash trade settles at 2:30 P.M. of the trade date. Transactions done after 2:00 P.M. settle 30 minutes later.

CHAPTER TWO

1. c Excess over Regulation T may be withdrawn or converted into buying power, enabling the customer to purchase additional securities.

2. d The debit balance is the amount of money the customer owes the brokerage firm.

3. c When the margin requirements are at 50 percent, the loan value or the amount the broker is permitted to finance is also 50 percent. Should the Federal Reserve increase the margin requirement to 60 percent, the loan value would only be 40 percent.

4. a Seven business days after the trade date. Payment for purchases in cash and margin accounts are the same.

5. d All of the ways indicated may be used to meet a margin call.

6. b $7,500—50 percent of the market value = $20,000 minus the customer's equity of $27,500 = $7,500 excess over Regulation T.

7. c Buying power at the 50 percent initial requirement is simply double the excess of $7,500, or $15,000.

Answers to Chapter Questions

8. **b** When the equity in a customer's margin account is below the existing margin requirement, the account is known as restricted margin account.

9. **b** $23,500. Any time there is a purchase in a customer's account the market value and the debit balance are increased by the full purchase price.

10. **d** Since there was no excess in this customer's account, a call for 50 percent of the purchase price—$4,250—would be made.

CHAPTER THREE

1. **d** As indicated in the chapter, many firms have *house requirements* that are higher than the NYSE minimum maintenance requirement. Consequently, a request by the broker for additional funds due to a market decline is a maintenance call.

2. **a** The NYSE minimum maintenance requirement is 25 percent of the market value of the long positions in the customer's account.

3. **c** When the equity exceeds the requirement of the NYSE. It may not be withdrawn or used as buying power. This excess simply means that the account may sustain even further market decline.

4. **c** A previously mentioned, excess over NYSE equity may not be withdrawn.

5. **d** While the requirement for Regulation T is 50 percent or $1,200, the NYSE initial requirement of $2,000, being greater, takes precedent.

6. **b** 25 percent of the current market value is $4,500, the equity is only $4,100; the customer would be on call for $400.

7. **a** To meet a NYSE minimum maintenance margin call by liquidation, you must sell four times the call $400 = $1,600.

8. **d** Purchases or sales without deposits or withdrawals do not change the equity in the customer's accounts.

9. a When meeting a maintenance call by bringing in additional securities, you must bring in 4/3 of $800—$1,067.

10. c Fifteen business days; this is the maximum amount of time.

CHAPTER FOUR

1. d The primary pupose of the SMA is to preserve the customer's buying power.

2. a Withdrawal of funds from the SMA will always increase the debit balance in the customer's margin account.

3. b Monies deposited to meet an outstanding Regulation T call will not affect the SMA. Deposits not required for Regulation T will increase the credit in the SMA.

4. c 50 percent of the current market value is the present loan value of listed securities that may be placed in the customer's SMA.

5. d Monies may always be withdrawn as long as the withdrawal does not put the account below the NYSE minimum maintenance requirement.

6. a Credit the SMA $10,000. While it is true that the customer's debit balance will be reduced by the $10,000 deposit, the debit balance is in the customer's margin account, not the SMA.

7. b Credit the SMA $750. Since the funds were not needed for Regulation T purposes, a credit of $750 to the SMA would be proper.

8. c A withdrawal from the SMA while the margin account is on NYSE call will only put the account on call further. No entry to the SMA; the request is improper.

9. a Again, the money received was not required by Regulation T; therefore, a credit to the SMA would be proper.

10. d The only time you could credit the SMA is when the excess is greater than the SMA balance, e.g., excess in a customer's

Answers to Chapter Questions

margin account $5,000, balance in the SMA $3,000. A credit of $2,000 to bring the SMA equal to the excess would be permitted.

CHAPTER FIVE

1. d All of the above statements are correct. You must be in a position to borrow the securities involved. In other words, you should not fail to deliver on a short sale. All sell orders must be specified as to either long or short. And last, in the event the security is listed on a national securities exchange, you are subject to the up-tick requirement.

2. b The NYSE minimum maintenance requirement for securities selling below $5.00 per share is $2.50 per share or 100 percent of the market value, whichever amount is greater. In our example, the customer is short 1,000 of ABC at $1.00. The requirement is $2,500.

3. d Regulation T says to treat the short sale as if it were long and release 50 percent to the customer. Consequently, there is no deposit required.

4. a The covering of a short sale releases the 50 percent of the current market value, the short sale closed out at $7,500. Therefore, the customer may withdraw $3,750.

5. b The NYSE requirement is $5.00 per share or 30 percent of the market value, whichever is greater. In this case, the 30 percent margin.

6. a $25,000—equity equals short market value—credit balance, in our example, the customer would have two credit balances—one in the margin account, the other in the short account.

7. d A restricted margin account. Short market value—credit balance.

8. c 36 ½, 36 ⅝, 36 ⅝, 36 ½.

9. b In this case, you are covered by the NYSE, and you are required to deposit (b) $2,000 even if this puts the account in excess of Regulation T.
10. c 150 shares, by definition.

CHAPTER SIX

1. d 25 percent; listed convertible bonds are treated the same as listed equity securities.
2. d A Treasury bill is classified as an *exempt* security.
3. a 15 percent of the market value or 7 percent of the principal amount, whichever is greater.
4. b 98 percent of the market value.
5. d All of the above are classified as exempt securities as defined by section 2 (12) of the Securities Exchange Act of 1934.
6. a 100 percent of the market value. Municipal revenue bonds are not eligible for margin: general obligations are eligible.
7. c The next business day is the normal settlement date, although special arrangements may be made such as two business days, etc.
8. b 3 percent of principal or 6 percent of the market value, whichever is greater.
9. a Foreign sovereign debt is to be treated the same as marginable corporate debt.
10. c The ratings must be one of the two highest ratings, AAA or AA.

CHAPTER SEVEN

1. b $2,000. The New York Stock Exchange has an initial requirement for opening a margin account of $2,000.

Answers to Chapter Questions

2. c $1,500. Monies in the SMA are on a dollar basis for meeting Regulation T calls. A purchase of $9,000 of listed securities requires $4,500. 50 percent of $9,000 less the $3,000 in the customer's SMA, or Reg. T call of $1,500.

3. a $3,000. A depopsit of $3,000 of listed securities has a loan value of $1,500 (50 percent of $3,000 = $1,500). A simple formula: twice the amount of the call must be deposited when the initial requirements are 50 percent.

4. a   Customer's margin account after the short sale and the appropriate deposit.

Margin Account	Short Account
$2,500 credit	Market value $5,000
	Credit balance 5,000

After the mark to the market:

Margin Account	Short Account
$2000 credit	Market value $5,500
	Credit balance 5,500

The increase in the credit balance in the customer's short account was occasioned by sending the lender the additional $500 so that the lender of the securities would have 100 percent of the market value of the securities being loaned.

5. d   The 90-day freeze requires the customer to have the necessary funds on hand before the purchase. Sales of securities are in no way affected by this restriction.

6. a $22,300 is the equity in this account. Subtract the debit balance from the market value to arrive at the customer's equity.

7. b $6,425

Req.	Eq.
$15,875	$22,300
	−15,875
	6,425

The requirement of $15,875 which is 25 percent of the market value less the customer's equity yields the maintenance excess.

8. a $15,875. The maintenance requirement is computed by taking 25 percent of the current market value: 25% × $63,500 = $15,875.

9. d $6,000. Remember the initial requirement for this example is 70 percent. In this account the equity is $48,000.

Req.	Eq.
$42,000	$48,000
	−42,000
	6,000 excess over Reg. T

10. b $8,571 would be the amount of securities that the customer could purchase without depositing any additional funds. The formula for arriving at the buying power is this: take the excess ($6,000), add a zero ($60,000) and divide by 7:

$$\frac{\$60,000}{7} = \$8,571$$

11. c The Federal Reserve. The Securities Exchange Act of 1934 gave the power to regulate credit on securities to the Federal Reserve.

12. d $500. The maintenance requirement is 25 percent of the market value ($2,500). The equity is only $2,000, so an additional $500 is required. The SMA of $5,000 would have no bearing in this example.

13. c $2,000. When meeting a maintenance call by liquidation, four times the amount of the call must be liquidated to meet the requirement. After the liquidation, the account would look like this:

Market value	$8,000
Debit balance	6,000
Equity	2,000

Answers to Chapter Questions

14. **b** The Securities Exchange Act of 1934.

15. **d** I and III. Securities traded on any national securities exchange or on the list published by the Federal Reserve called the over-the-counter marginable list.

16. **a** $5,000. When the requirement is 50 percent, 50 percent may be released on the sale of a listed security in a restricted margin account.

17. **c** Any day that the exchanges are open.

18. **b** $2,500. The initial requirement for Regulation T is $1,000 (50 percent of the market value) However, the NYSE minimum equity requirement is $2.50 per share or 100 percent whichever is greater. In this case, $2,500 is greater.

19. **d** $680. The requirements are 15 percent of the market value, which would mean the security would have a loan value of 85 percent or $680. Market value of this bond is 80 percent of $1,000, or $800.

20. **c** The new requirements effective September 1, 1987, are 5 percent of the market value, keeping the short side marked to the market.

21. **d** All of these securities are exempt securities.

22. **b** No. Treasury bills are no longer a physical security. They are recorded in the Federal Reserve's book entry system.

23. **b** Must be segregated and identified as belonging to the customer.

24. **c** The New York Stock Exchange. Although it is the Federal Reserve rule to obtain an extension, it is the various exchanges and the NASD that grant or deny extensions.

25. **b** $1,500. A purchase of $9,000 and a sale of $12,000 leaves a net sale of $3,000. 50 percent of $3,000 = $1,500 even in a restricted margin account.

Appendix C

GLOSSARY

ACCRUED INTEREST—The interest owed by the buyer to the seller of bonds because that individual held the bond for a portion of the next interest payment. Interest accrues up to, but not including, the settlement date.

ADR—American depository receipt. A receipt for foreign securities being held in the country of origin by an American bank. This instrument facilitates the trading of foreign securities.

ARBITRAGE—The purchase of one security and the subsequent sale of the same security, either long or short, to take advantage of the price spread in the marketplace.

BABY BOND—A bond with a face value of less than $1,000. The vast majority of bonds have a face value payable at maturity of $1,000. Most baby bonds are for a face value of $500.

BEARER BONDS—Bonds that are not registered in the owner's name. The holder is the owner. Since July 1983, any new municipal bond issued has to be registered. While bearer bonds will eventually become extinct, a number of them are still around.

BOND—An instrument representing debt by the issuer to be paid to the holder. Bonds are quoted as a percentage of par ($1,000). Therefore, a bond being quoted as selling at 80 ½ is selling at 80.5 percent of $1,000, or $805.

BOX—The Box is an old term referring to the time when all physical securities were held in the possession of the broker. There are now several boxes—e.g., active box, free box, safekeeping (usually meaning the securities are held with the Depository Trust Company).

BUSINESS DAY—The best definition of a business day is one on which the New York Stock Exchange is open. This always causes confusion, since there are certain days that the banks are closed but the exchanges are open (Martin Luther King's Birthday, Veteran's Day and Columbus Day) and others that banks are open and the exchanges are closed (Good Friday).

BUY IN—Occurs when securities have been purchased, but not delivered on time. The receiving broker goes into the market, buys the securities, and any loss is passed on to the firm failing to deliver the securities.

CAGE—The area in a brokerage firm where the securities are held, received, and delivered out. Years ago, as a security precaution, this area was literally fenced off. Today much more elaborate security devices exist.

CALLABLE—A feature of certain preferred stocks and bonds. This feature gives the issuer the right to call the security to redeem or retire the issue prior to the original maturity date. If bonds were issued when interest rates were very high, it would be prudent to issue callable bonds so they could be called, then refinanced if rates drop in the future.

CALL LOAN—A loan to be paid back upon demand by the lender. Brokers borrow money from banks at the broker's call rate, which is a secured demand borrowing.

Glossary

CASHIERS DEPARTMENT—A more refined term for the cage; the department responsible for movement of securities and monies.

CASH ON DELIVERY—C.O.D. transactions are usually used by institutions to settle buy transactions. For example, ABC Pension Fund purchases 10,000 shares of IBM for $1,250,000 and issues instructions to deliver versus payment to ABC Pension Fund's bank.

COMMINGLING—Mixing customer's securities that are fully paid for with those that are being financed. This is a violation of rules.

COMMON STOCK—An equity security in a corporation representing an ownership interest and carrying rights such as the right to vote and share in the profits. These shares are easily transferable.

COVER—The term used to describe closing out a short position, either by buying the security in the open market and returning it to the lender and/or delivering your long position against the short position.

CREDIT BALANCE—Free credit balance monies belonging to the customer. Ledger credit balance monies obtained as a result of the proceeds of the short sale and being used as collateral for the stock loan.

CURRENT MARKET VALUE—(1) The actual price paid when purchasing or received when selling securities. (2) When valuing securities in an account, it is the closing price of the previous day, as shown by any regularly published reporting or quotation service.

DAY TRADE—The purchase and sale of a security on the same day. There is no position in the security at the end of the day, either long or short; therefore, there is no initial Regulation T requirement.

DEBIT BALANCE—The amount of money the customer owes the brokerage firm.

DELIVERY AGAINST PAYMENT—Regulation T description of a C.O.D. transaction.

DISCOUNT RATE—The rate at which the Federal Reserve will lend its member banks on a secured basis. The proceeds may only be used to meet the reserve requirement of the Federal Reserve.

DISCOUNT WINDOW—The location where members of the Federal Reserve borrow at the discount rate.

DON'T KNOW—DK is the term used when a broker or bank rejects a delivery of securities because the transaction is literally not known to them.

DOWN TICK— The previous sale was higher than the present sale. For example, 10 ½ 10 ⅜ , the price 10 ⅜ represents a down tick. If a customer wanted to sell short at this price, the short sale would be prohibited. Short sales of listed securities may be made only on an up tick or zero-plus tick.

EQUITY—Represents the customer's ownership in the account. If the customer sold all the securities and paid all the debts, what would be left is the equity.

EQUITY SECURITY—Represents ownership as opposed to debt. Common stock and preferred stocks are the most common equity securities.

EXCESS MARGIN—That amount of equity in an account above the amount required by the Federal Reserve for initial requirements or by the New York Stock Exchange for minimum maintenance requirements.

EXEMPT SECURITIES—Direct obligations of the United States government—Treasury bills, notes and bonds; obligations of agencies that are guaranteed as to principal and/or interest by the United States government; and obligations of any political subdivision of the United States (municipal securities). These are exempt from registration with the SEC and exempt from Regulation T of the Federal Reserve.

FACE VALUE—The principal amount. The face value dollar amount payable at maturity for most bonds is $1,000.

FAIL TO DELIVER—The selling broker does not deliver the security by settlement date to the buying broker.

FAIL TO RECEIVE—The buying broker does not receive the purchased securities by settlement date from the selling broker.

FEDERAL FUNDS—Funds bought and sold by banks to deposit at the Federal Reserve to meet their reserve requirements.

FEDERAL FUND RATE—The rate at which Federal Funds trade. The variations are caused strictly by supply and demand.

FEDERAL RESERVE BOARD—Seven governors all appointed by the President of the United States for 14-year terms.

FED WIRE—One of the advantages of being a member of the Federal Reserve System is access to the Fed wire which moves funds from one member bank to another member bank on the same day.

FREE FUNDS LETTER—The letter that is required to be obtained when delivering purchased securities for payment from the receiving broker. It states that these funds do not represent the proceeds of the sale of that security.

FREE RIDING—Under Regulation T, it refers to purchasing a security and selling it prior to making full payment. This practice is prohibited.

FROZEN ACCOUNT—A cash account in which the customer has purchased a security and sold the same security without making full cash payment. During this frozen period (90 calendar days), purchases may be made only if funds sufficient for the full amount of the purchase are already in the account.

GENERAL ACCOUNT—The old terminology for a margin account. When Regulation T was revised in 1983, *general account* was replaced by *margin account.*

GENERAL OBLIGATION—A type of municipal security on which credit may be extended. Revenue bonds are not eligible for the margin account.

GUARANTEED ACCOUNT—Where one account is guaranteed by another for meeting the New York Stock Exchange minimum maintenance requirements.

HOUSE RULES—Any rule by the broker that increases the requirements of the Federal Reserve or the New York Stock Exchange. For example, NYSE minimum maintenance requirements are 25 percent of the current market value. The broker may require 30 percent of the market value.

HYPOTHECATION AGREEMENT—An agreement signed by the customer that the securities in the margin account are not held in the customer's name and may be pledged to finance the customer's debit balance.

INITIAL MARGIN—Usually thought of as the initial requirement of Regulation T, which is currently 50 percent of the purchase price. Additionally, the New York Stock Exchange requires an initial margin of $2,000 to open a margin account.

LISTED STOCK—Any security traded on a National Securities Exchange:
  New York Stock Exchange
  American Stock Exchange
  Boston Stock Exchange
  Philadelphia Stock Exchange
  Midwest Stock Exchange

Glossary

Cincinnati Stock Exchange
Pacific Coast Stock Exchange

The Honolulu Stock Exchange is classified as an exempt exchange, but the securities traded there are also considered listed securities.

LOAN VALUE—The amount of money a broker may extend on listed securities. The Reg. T requirement at this time is 50 percent; therefore the loan value is 50 percent. If the Federal Reserve raises the Reg. T requirement to 70 percent of the market value, the loan value would be 30 percent.

LONG—Securities that are physically in the customer's account.

MAINTENANCE CALL—When a customer is notified that an amount of money must be deposited to maintain his margin account.

MAINTENANCE REQUIREMENT—The amount of money necessary to maintain a customer's margin account. New York Stock Exchange requires a customer to maintain a minimum of 25 percent of the current market value.

MARGIN CALL—A request for additional funds. It may be a maintenance call, but usually refers to the initial requirement of the Federal Reserve.

MARGIN DEPARTMENT—The department in the brokerage firm that is responsible for maintaining the customer's account, insuring compliance with the rules of the Federal Reserve, the Securities and Exchange Commission, the New York Stock Exchange, and the firm's own house policies.

MARGIN REQUIREMENT—The initial requirement set by the Federal Reserve in Regulation T.

MARGIN SECURITY—A security that a broker may extend loan value or credit on, including listed securities (meaning those traded on any national securities exchange). Those OTC securities on the list published by the Federal Reserve known as the over-the-counter marginable list, any open end mutual fund, or any security qualified for trading in the National Market System.

MARK TO THE MARKET—Changing securities prices to reflect the current market values along with the appropriate debit or credit.

MUNICIPAL SECURITIES—Securities issued by "political subdivisions of the United States," better known as states, cities, counties, and towns. There are two types of municipal securities: general obligations and revenue bonds. General obligations are backed by the full faith and credit of the municipality. Revenue bonds are backed by the revenue generated by the particular facility and in the event the revenues are not sufficient to repay the interest or principal, the bonds go into default.

NASD—National Association of Securities Dealers. Founded in 1939 and granted authority to regulate their members and the over-the-counter market similar to the authority the stock exchanges have in regulating their members and their markets.

NON-PURPOSE LOAN—The old name for the Non-Securities Credit Account. Revision of Regulation T in 1983 changed the name.

NON-SECURITIES CREDIT ACCOUNT—This account allows the broker to extend credit to a customer on a secured or nonsecured basis if the purpose of the loan is for something other than purchasing or carrying securities, for instance, the payment of taxes, purchasing a boat, or taking a vacation. While the Federal Reserve allows 100 percent credit on securities, members of the New York Stock Exchange are only allowed to extend 75 percent loan value. The remaining 25 percent is the New York Stock Exchange minimum maintenance requirement.

OTC MARGIN STOCK—Securities traded in the over-the-counter market but placed on a list published by the Federal Reserve Board that allows a broker to extend credit at the 50 percent level as he may on listed securities.

PARTIAL DELIVERY—Delivery of only a part of the total shares bought.

PLUS TICK—The present sale is higher than the previous sale. For example, 10 ⅞ 11, the price 11 represents a plus tick. Short sales of listed securities may only be made on an up tick or zero-plus tick.

RECEIVE VERSUS PAYMENT—Delivery of securities to a broker or agent who has been instructed to make payment of the proceeds of the sale upon receipt.

REGISTERED REPRESENTATIVE—A broker who is licensed to purchase and sell securities. He/she is registered to represent the brokerage firm.

REGISTERED SECURITY—Under Regulation T, any margin security. Under the Securities Act of 1933, any security that has been registered with the Securities Exchange Commission.

REGULAR WAY SETTLEMENT—The security settles five business days from the trade date.

REGULAR WAY TRANSACTION—A security transaction done for Regular Way settlement.

REGULATION G—Federal Reserve regulation that governs the amount of credit a nonbroker or nonbank may extend on securities.

REGULATION T—Federal Reserve regulation that governs the amount of credit a broker may extend on securities.

REGULATION U—Federal Reserve regulation that governs the amount of credit a bank may extend on securities.

REGULATION W—Federal Reserve regulation that governs the amount of credit that may be extended on household appliances, etc.

REHYPOTHECATION—When a customer pledges securities to obtain a margin loan from a broker, the broker repledges them with a bank to finance the debit balance.

REJECTION—A delivery of securities is made versus payment and the delivery is turned down or rejected. Many times this is referred to as a DK. In reality, the DK is the reason for the rejection.

RESERVE REQUIREMENT—The amount of funds that must be deposited with the Federal Reserve, depending on the size of the bank's demand deposit accounts, savings accounts, and time deposits.

RESTRICTED ACCOUNT—A margin account where the equity is below the existing margin requirement. For example, with the current requirement at 50 percent the following margin account would be restricted:

Market value	$10,000
Debit balance	6,000
Equity	4,000

RETENTION REQUIREMENT—The amount that must be withheld on the sale of securities in a restricted margin account.

REVENUE BOND—A municipal security that will repay principal and interest as a result of the revenue generated by the particular facility.

SAFEKEEPING—Customers' fully paid-for securities or securities representing more than 140 percent of the customers' debit balance are kept segregated from all others.

Glossary

SECURITIES LOAN—Securities that are loaned to facilitate a short sale.

SEGREGATE—See Safekeeping.

SETTLEMENT DATE—The date when securities are delivered in settlement of a sale, or the date money is due for a purchase. On most securities transactions, it is five business days after the trade date. On U.S. government obligations, the normal settlement date is the next business day.

SHORT VERSUS THE BOX—The short sale of the securities that the customer is long, done for tax reasons or to lock in a profit or loss.

SHORT EXEMPT—The sale of a security on a down tick. May be done in an arbitrage situation.

STOCK RECORD—A record used by brokers to list the positions, locations, and owners of securities.

TREASURY BILL—A debt instrument of the U.S. government that matures in one year or less and is traded on a discount basis. Denominations run from $10,000 to $1 million.

TREASURY BOND—Long-term debt instrument of the U.S. government—from 10 to 35 years maturity. Denominations run from $1,000 to $1 million.

TREASURY NOTE—Medium-term debt instrument of the U.S. government—from one to ten years maturity. Denominations run from $1,000 to $500 million.

UNLISTED SECURITIES—Securities not traded on a national securities exchange, more commonly known as over-the-counter securities.

WHEN-DISTRIBUTED—A security that is issued, but not yet distributed; for instance, if a company owns another company and is going to distribute the shares to its stockholders. Before the securities can be physically distributed, they may trade on a when-distributed basis.

WHEN ISSUED—A security that has not been issued, but is traded on a when- as- and- if-issued basis.

ZERO-MINUS TICK—A situation in which the previous sale is the same as the current one but is down from the last different one. For example, 10 ½ 10 ¼ 10 ¼—the first 10 ¼ is a down or minus tick, the second 10 ¼ is a zero-minus tick.

ZERO-PLUS TICK—A situation where the previous sale is the same as the current one but is up from the last different one. For example, 10 ½ 10 ⅝ 10 ⅝—the first 10 ⅝ is a plus or up tick, the second 10 ⅝ is a zero-plus tick.

ABOUT THE AUTHOR

Michael T. Curley began his Wall Street career nearly twenty years ago with the New York Stock Exchange, and has remained in the forefront of broker training and education ever since. Currently, Mr. Curley is Vice-President of Wall Street Training & Consulting, Inc., as well as a faculty member of the New York Institute of Finance. His broad range of experience includes serving as the Manager of Brokerage Operations for Citibank.

Mr. Curley is a graduate of Aldelphi University and lives in New York City.